Lectures on Philosophical Theology

Also by Allen W. Wood

Kant's Moral Religion
Kant's Rational Theology

IMMANUEL KANT

Lectures on Philosophical Theology

Translated by
Allen W. Wood and **Gertrude M. Clark**
with introduction and notes by Allen W. Wood

Cornell University Press Ithaca and London

First published 1978 by Cornell University Press.
Second printing, 1982.
First printing, Cornell Paperbacks, 1986.

International Standard Book Number (cloth) 0-8014-1199-8
International Standard Book Number (paper) 0-8014-9379-X
Library of Congress Catalog Card Number 78-58034
Printed in the United States of America
Librarians: Library of Congress cataloging information appears on the last page of the book.

The paper in this book is acid free, and meets the guidelines for permanence and durability of the Committee on Production Guidelines for Book Longevity of the Council on Library Resources.

TO HENRY

Contents

Translator's Introduction

Kant's lectures at the University of Königsberg have been preserved for us in a variety of forms, through notes and auditors' transcriptions. Most of this material merely expounds doctrines that are familiar to us from Kant's published writings, and recommends itself chiefly on account of the relatively popular form in which Kant presented his philosophy. In Kant's published writings on the subject of philosophical theology, we certainly find full and definitive accounts of many things discussed in the lectures: the rational origin of the idea of God, the moral arguments for faith, the Kantian criticism of the traditional theistic proofs. On this last point, in fact, the lectures contain very little that is new, and in many places merely parrot the *Critique of Pure Reason*. Yet on several other points, the *Lectures on Philosophical Theology* are uniquely informative. In them, the difficult argument presented in Chapter II of the Ideal of Pure Reason is presented in a much less stiff and scholastic manner; Kant's philosophical motivations are much clearer. And these lectures contain an unusually large amount of material that is not dealt with explicitly elsewhere in the Kantian corpus. They provide us with the only statement (except for very brief hints in the *Nachlass* fragments) of the illuminating "*absurdum practicum*" version of Kant's moral argument for theism.[1] They reveal more

1. See Allen W. Wood, *Kant's Moral Religion* (Ithaca, N.Y.: 1970), pp. 25–34; cf. *Gesammelte Schriften*, Berlin Akademie Ausgabe, vol. 18, pp. 19, 26, 193f. But

familiarity with Hume's *Dialogues concerning Natural Religion* than does any other of Kant's writings. And Kant's treatments of physicotheology, theodicy, and the evil in human nature compare interestingly with his later published views on these subjects.[2]

But most important, the *Lectures on Philosophical Theology* are our main source for Kant's views on many of the traditional issues of philosophical theology: the nature and attributes of God, God's relation to the world, God's causality, creation, and divine providence. And they show, perhaps surprisingly, that despite Kant's generally critical stance toward the transcendent metaphysics of the scholastics and rationalists, he remained quite sympathetic to traditional theology on many points.

In translating these lectures, we have tried to be as straightforward and literal as possible, in order to capture the simplicity and directness of style that distinguish them from most of Kant's published works. We have also attempted to achieve transparency and strict consistency in translating philosophical terminology, though we have chosen not to do so in a few cases (for example, in rendering the terms *Verbindung*, *Verknüpfung*, and *Zusammensetzung*) where the inconsistency seemed to involve no philosophical loss, and where consistency would have been bought at the price of smooth and intelligible English. In these lectures, Kant is often commenting on specific passages in Baumgarten, and most of the footnotes aim at helping the reader to catch allusions of which Kant's audience would certainly have been aware. A few footnotes attempt to expound or clarify Kant's meaning, or comment on what he is saying; but this practice has been kept to a minimum. For more extended discussion of some of the main themes in these lectures, see my *Kant's Moral Religion* and *Kant's Rational Theology*.

The Text of the Lectures

Kant lectured on a wide variety of subjects in the course of his teaching duties at the University of Königsberg. During his fif-

---

see also Pölitz's edition of *Immanuel Kants Vorlesungen über Metaphysik* (Erfurt, 1821), p. 298; cf. *Gesammelte Schriften*, vol. 28, 1, p. 319.

2. On the topic of theodicy, compare Kant's 1791 essay "Uber das Misslingen

teen years as *Privatdozent*, when his livelihood depended entirely on student fees, and consequently on the popularity of what he taught, the philosopher frequently found himself reading not only on mathematics, physics, and geography, but even on such subjects as military fortification and pyrotechnics.[3] After Kant's appointment to a professorship in 1770, the scope of his teaching narrowed somewhat, but continued to reflect his extraordinary breadth of learning and scientific interest.

Four works based on these lectures were published before Kant's death in 1804. The philosopher himself edited *Anthropology from a Pragmatic Standpoint*, published in 1798. Two years later, his disciple Gottlob Benjamin Jäsche brought out the lectures on logic. Another younger colleague, Friedrich Theodor Rink, subsequently issued Kant's lectures on physical geography and education, in 1802 and 1803 respectively. These editions were based both on manuscripts by Kant and on transcriptions of lectures by his students. Jäsche and Rink worked with the full cooperation and approval of Kant, whose failing powers made it impossible for him to complete the editions himself.

Rink and Jäsche apparently intended to publish a number of other such books, based on Kant's lectures. But almost simultaneously with Rink's edition of the geography lectures, there appeared another version of them that was prepared by the Mainz publisher Gottfried Vollmer, and that claimed to be "the legitimate edition" of the same material. Since Kant had earlier denied Vollmer permission to issue the geography lectures, Rink responded angrily in print to Vollmer's "insinuations" about the authenticity of his own edition. A bitter controversy ensued, with the result that Rink abandoned his intention of publishing the other lecture manuscripts he possessed. In his preface to the lectures on education, he wrote, somewhat petulantly: "After the base attacks which the bookdealer Vollmer allowed himself on my edition of the Kantian physical geography, it is no longer possible for the editing of such manuscripts

---

aller philosophische Versuche in der Theodicee," *Gesammelte Schriften*, vol. 8, pp. 253–272. On radical evil, compare the essay on that subject in Kant's *Religion within the Limits of Reason Alone* (1793).

3. J. H. W. Stuckenberg, *The Life of Immanuel Kant* (London, 1882), pp. 68f.

to be a pleasant business for me. Since I can live peacefully, contented and busy within my own sphere of activity (which even without this is by no means narrow), why should I lower myself to making unasked for claims, and abandon myself to untimely judgments?"[4]

In 1817, six years after Rink's death, a set of Kant's lectures on rational theology appeared under the title *Immanuel Kants Vorlesungen über die philosophische Religionslehre*, edited by the Leipzig Kantian Karl Heinrich Ludwig Pölitz. Four years later, Pölitz published an edition of Kant's lectures on metaphysics, and in 1830 he brought out a new edition of the theology lectures. The present translation is based on the text of this second edition.

In the preface to his first edition of the lectures, Pölitz asserted that his text was a "careful verbal transcription" of Kant's own words, which he was publishing unaltered, and which he had obtained by purchase from the estate of a "formerly respected and now deceased colleague of Kant at Königsberg." In the preface to the 1830 edition, Pölitz finally identified Rink as the previous owner of the manuscripts and conjectured that, as the theology lectures possessed a "higher inner worth" than those on either geography or education, only Rink's premature death had prevented him from publishing them eventually himself.[5]

It is difficult to know just how far to credit Pölitz's account of the nature and origin of his source. In 1972, the Pölitz text was republished in the Akademie edition of Kant's writings, along with three related (but shorter and rather fragmentary) manuscript versions of Kant's lectures on rational theology. The latest editor, Gerhard Lehmann, is somewhat skeptical of Pölitz's account generally and seems to think that Pölitz's text represents a synthesis of these more fragmentary versions.[6] Yet it must

4. *Gesammelte Schriften*, vol. 9, p. 440. Cf. ibid., pp. 510ff.

5. *Vorlesungen über die philosophische Religionslehre* (Leipzig, 1830), pp. v, ix. Cf. *Gesammelte Schriften*, vol. 28, 2, 2, pp. 1511ff.

6. *Gesammelte Schriften*, vol. 28, 2, 2, p. 1361. Cf. Kurt Beyer, *Kants Vorlesungen über die philosophische Religionslehre* (Halle, 1937). The other three versions of the lectures are: (1) a manuscript of notes bearing the name Johann Wilhelm Volckmann, dated November 13, 1783, 98 pages in length (when printed); cf. *Gesammelte Schriften*, vol. 28, 2, 2, pp. 1127–1225; (2) an anonymous manuscript, dated July 19, 1784, found in the Danzig municipal library, 92 pages in length

have been based on some material that is no longer extant, since it is considerably longer than any of the manuscript versions, and its wording deviates considerably from theirs. There seems to be no good reason, in any case, for doubting that Pölitz's source or sources came from Rink's posthumous papers.

More generally, the doctrines contained in these lectures, whenever we can compare them with Kant's published works, appear to be authentically Kantian and authentically critical. It is true that in a few cases (such as the surprisingly sympathetic treatments of physicotheology and of Kant's own 1763 proof for God's existence) there might seem to be a tension between the lectures and the *Critique of Pure Reason*. But I am inclined to regard the lectures at such points as supplementing rather than contradicting what is said in the first critique; and the specific additions strike me as natural ones for Kant to have made in adapting his philosophy to classroom presentation. On the whole, the principled philological skepticism with which one always approaches a text of this kind provides us in this case with no very good grounds for doubting that Pölitz's record represents a tolerably faithful account of the views Kant held at the time he gave the lectures on which it is based.

In Kant's day, professors were required to lecture on a set text. In the theology lectures, Kant is commenting on two different books: first, the *Vorbereitung zur natürlichen Theologie* by the Halle philosopher Johann August Eberhard, who was later to be Kant's opponent in a controversy on the relation of the critical philosophy to Leibnizian rationalism;[7] and second, the treatise of natural theology contained in Part III of the *Metaphysica* of Alexander Gottlieb Baumgarten. The *Metaphysica* was one of the standard works of Wolffian rationalism and the text used regularly by Kant in his courses on metaphysics. The Eberhard textbook is a work of much less philosophical interest, and Kant's discussion of it is accordingly brief, as well as more distant and cursory.

(when printed); cf. *Gesammelte Schriften*, vol. 28, 2, 2, pp. 1227–1319; and (3) a brief, undated fragment, 10 pages in length (when printed); cf. *Gesammelte Schriften*, vol. 28, 2, 2, pp. 1321–1331.

7. See Henry E. Allison, ed., *The Kant-Eberhard Controversy* (Baltimore, 1973).

The organization of the lectures in Pölitz's text in no way indicates the separation of the particular lectures from each other. On this point, Pölitz merely followed the practice of Kant, Rink, and Jäsche in their earlier editions of Kantian lectures. From the end of Kant's discussion of the three theistic proofs onward, his order of presentation appears to have been dictated more by the order of paragraphs in Baumgarten than by anything else, so that the divisions in Pölitz's edition are to some extent an arbitrary form imposed on what is—with a few interruptions and digressions—largely a running commentary on the *Metaphysica*. And of course in the end it is impossible to distinguish clearly the contributions of Pölitz and of Kant's transcriber from whatever principles of organization Kant may have intended himself. Pölitz does not indicate how the curious appendix dealing with Meiners' early book on the history of religions is related to Kant's lectures on the other two textbooks.

Just when did Kant deliver these lectures? Pölitz says that although his manuscript bears no date, "it can be concluded from external criteria that it was transcribed in the first years of the ninth decade of the previous century."[8] Pölitz does not elaborate on this, but some internal evidence can be presented in favor of his estimate. The lectures cannot have predated 1781, for this was the year in which Eberhard's *Vorbereitung* was first published; it was also the first year in which Kant could have had access to a German translation of Hume's *Dialogues*, of which the lectures exhibit a fairly detailed knowledge. They certainly postdate the first edition of the *Critique of Pure Reason* (1781), and in fact contain a few passages that seem to be taken from it almost verbatim. There are also one or two places where the text closely resembles that of the *Prolegomena* of 1783. The contents of the lectures give us less by which to fix their date in the other direction; but Kant's account of the principle of morality as "the agreement of an action with the idea of a system" is one which very likely antedates the *Grundlegung* of 1785.[9]

8. *Vorlesungen*, p. xvi; cf. *Gesammelte Schriften*, vol. 28, 2, 2, p. 1518.

9. Regarding the availability of Hume's *Dialogues*, see *Gesammelte Schriften*, vol. 28, 2, 2, p. 1363. For parallels with the *Critique of Pure Reason*, see Kant's critique of ontotheology in the First Part. For one parallel with the *Prolegomena*,

Kant lectured regularly every winter semester on Baumgarten's *Metaphysica*, including the part on natural theology. But it was not often that he made philosophical theology as such his theme. In the late 1750s and early 1760s, during the Russian occupation of Königsberg, he apparently taught a course on Leibnizian optimism and delivered a series of lectures concerned with the criticism of traditional proofs for God's existence. During his critical period, however, Kant seems to have announced lectures on philosophical theology only once, in the winter of 1785–1786. But it is clear that he lectured on the subject at other times in the eighties. According to Kant's sometime friend Johann Georg Hamann, the philosopher lectured on theology to "an astonishing throng" in the winter semester of 1783–1784. And Reinhold Bernhard Jachmann, Kant's student in 1783 and later his amanuensis, reports that Kant's most enjoyable experience with the subject was an occasion when his hearers consisted almost entirely of theology students. Many of these "apostles," Jachmann tells us, "went forth and taught the gospel of the realm of pure reason."[10]

It is probable that Pölitz's source derives from Kant's first and most popular set of lectures, given in the winter of 1783–1784. Not only does internal evidence point this way, but so do the dates, 13 November 1783 and 19 July 1784, on the two extant manuscript versions. Erich Adickes was evidently convinced of the correctness of this date for the Pölitz lectures, since he used it as his principal basis for assigning the date 1783 to the material in Kant's *Nachlass* that pertains to Eberhard's *Vorbereitung*.[11]

---

see Kant's description of analogical predication. (Cf. *Vorlesungen*, p. 53; *Gesammelte Schriften*, vol. 28, 2, 2, p. 1023, and vol. 4, p. 357; cf. *Prolegomena to Any Future Metaphysics*, ed. L. W. Beck [Indianapolis, 1950], p. 106). On the formulation of the principle of morality, see below, Second Part, Third Section, and W. B. Waterman, "Kant's Lectures on the Philosophical Theory of Religion," *Kant-Studien* 2 (1899), 301–303.

10. On Kant's earliest theology lectures, see Karl Vorländer, *Immanuel Kant: Der Mann und das Werk* (Leipzig, 1924), vol. 2, pp. 10–15, and Stuckenberg, pp. 71f. The announced lectures are reported by Emil Arnoldt; see Waterman, "Kant's Lectures," p. 306. Hamann's remark is quoted by Vorländer, *Immanuel Kants Leben* (Leipzig, 1911), p. 121. Reinhold Bernhard Jachmann, *Immanuel Kant* (Königsberg, 1804).

11. *Gesammelte Schriften*, vol. 28, 2, 2, pp. 1129, 1229; vol. 18, p. 504.

Kant as Lecturer

The principal interest the *Lectures on Philosophical Theology* have for us must consist in the light they shed on Kant's views. But Kant's lectures have an irreplaceable value in that they show us a side of Kant as a philosopher that is usually quite hidden by the formality and infamously forbidding style of his published works. "Through them," wrote Pölitz, "we may convince ourselves how clear and comprehensible, how warm and emphatic, how ordered and connected, were Kant's oral presentations, and how the noble popularity of his lectures in many points surpasses the stylistic character of his writings for publication."[12]

According to the jurist Thibaut, Kant said more than once: "I do not read for geniuses, for they will by their own nature find their own road; nor for the stupid, for they are not worth the trouble; but rather for those who stand in between, and who would be educated for their future calling." As a lecturer, Kant had the reputation for being both witty and erudite, but nevertheless somewhat dry and difficult to follow for many students; his lectures on Baumgarten's *Metaphysica*, moreover, were regarded as his most abstruse and least popular. But Kant never pretended to be lecturing for beginners in philosophy, and he recommended to students that they prepare themselves for his lectures by first hearing those of his younger colleague, Professor Pörschke.[13]

It is difficult to form a clear picture of Kant's lecturing style from the reports that have come down to us. Rink is supposed to have been of the opinion that Kant's platform manner deteriorated markedly as he grew older, and that even by the late 1770s his lectures had lost most of the liveliness they once possessed. Jachmann, however, who heard Kant's lectures only in the eighties and nineties, gives a glowing account of them. Of the lectures on moral subjects, he says: "How often he moved us to tears, how often he forcibly shook our hearts, how often he

12. *Vorlesungen*, p. vi; cf. *Gesammelte Schriften*, vol. 28, 2, 2, p. 1515.

13. The quotation from Thibaut is reported by Vorländer, *Kants Leben*, p. 123. On the comparative abstruseness of Kant's lectures on Baumgarten's *Metaphysica*, see Vorländer, *Kants Leben*, p. 96, and Jachmann, pp. 28f.

raised our spirit and our feelings out of the fetters of selfish eudaimonism and up to the high self-consciousness of pure freedom of the will!" Even Kant's lectures on metaphysics, according to Jachmann, were, allowing for the difficulty of the subject matter, both clear and full of charm.[14]

From the year 1783 onward, Kant always gave his lectures in an auditorium on the ground floor of his home on Prinzessinstrasse in a centrally located but quiet part of Königsberg. The lecture room was rather small, and sometimes, when Kant's audiences were exceptionally large, the better part of them had to listen from the entry hall and other adjoining rooms. The lectures were always scheduled early in the morning: seven to nine four days of the week, and eight to ten Wednesdays and Saturdays. According to Jachmann, Kant was a "model of punctuality," not missing a lecture for over nine years, and always arriving on time, impeccably dressed *à la mode française*.[15]

The philosopher lectured sitting at a little desk, slightly elevated above his audience. As he spoke, Kant often selected one of those who were sitting closest to him and looked this student in the eye, as if to determine how well he was making himself understood. This habit could prove somewhat disconcerting to the student chosen. Kant was, moreover, very easily annoyed and distracted by personal peculiarities in his hearers. Even a button missing from a student's coat was sometimes sufficient to catch his eye repeatedly, disturbing his concentration. On one occasion, it is reported, a student expressed his weariness with the lecture by indulging in several long yawns. "If one cannot avoid yawning," said Kant pointedly, interrupting his lecture, "good manners require that the hand should be held before the mouth."[16]

Kant regularly spent the hour from six to seven in the morning preparing for his lectures. His presentation, however, was informal by the standards of the day. He seldom read material

14. Rink's view is reported by Stuckenberg, p. 82. But compare Jachmann, pp. 29–31.

15. Vorländer, *Kants Leben*, p. 138; Jachmann, pp. 33, 27, 164; Stuckenberg, p. 168f.

16. Jachmann, p. 34; cf. Stuckenberg, pp. 81f.

he had written out, but usually spoke from notes jotted in the margins of his copy of the textbook, or from a small sheet of paper he brought with him. Kant refused to confine himself to the usual practice of simply setting forth the position of the text on the issue at hand. He insisted on trying out various lines of thought, probing and testing them before the students. This method, it is said, is one reason that his lectures demanded a good deal of his hearers and could not be followed without considerable effort. Kant had a tendency to become fascinated by issues of particular difficulty or subtlety and to permit himself lengthy digressions in pursuit of them. Jachmann says that often when Kant caught himself wandering too far in this manner he would break off abruptly and, with the characteristic expression "*in summa, meine Herren,*" would return suddenly to the main point.[17]

On many serious students of philosophy, Kant's lectures made an overwhelming impression. "Of him," says Jachmann, "the proverb is not true that the prophet is not honored in his own country. For he was practically deified by his hearers, who seized every opportunity to prove this to him." Along with many of Kant's other contemporaries, however, he emphasized that the philosopher's aim was never to furnish his audiences with a ready-made doctrine, but to teach them to think for themselves. According to Borowski, Kant "would not teach philosophy, but rather philosophizing, thinking." For this reason, Kant discouraged students from taking detailed notes or attempting verbatim transcriptions of his lectures, such as the one here translated; he preferred them instead to pay close attention and to reflect critically on what he was saying. It sometimes annoyed him, in fact, to see students scribbling when he felt they should be thinking. Once the sound of students' pens so disturbed Kant that he broke off his discourse, remarking irritably: "Gentlemen, do not scratch so; I am no oracle."[18]

17. Jachmann, pp. 27–30, 164. Vorländer, *Kants Leben*, p. 122. Stuckenberg, p. 74.

18. Stuckenberg, p. 81. Ludwig Ernst Borowski, *Darstellung des Lebens und Characters Immanuel Kants* (Königsberg, 1804), p. 84; cf. Vorländer, *Kants Leben*, p. 47, Jachmann, pp. 35f.

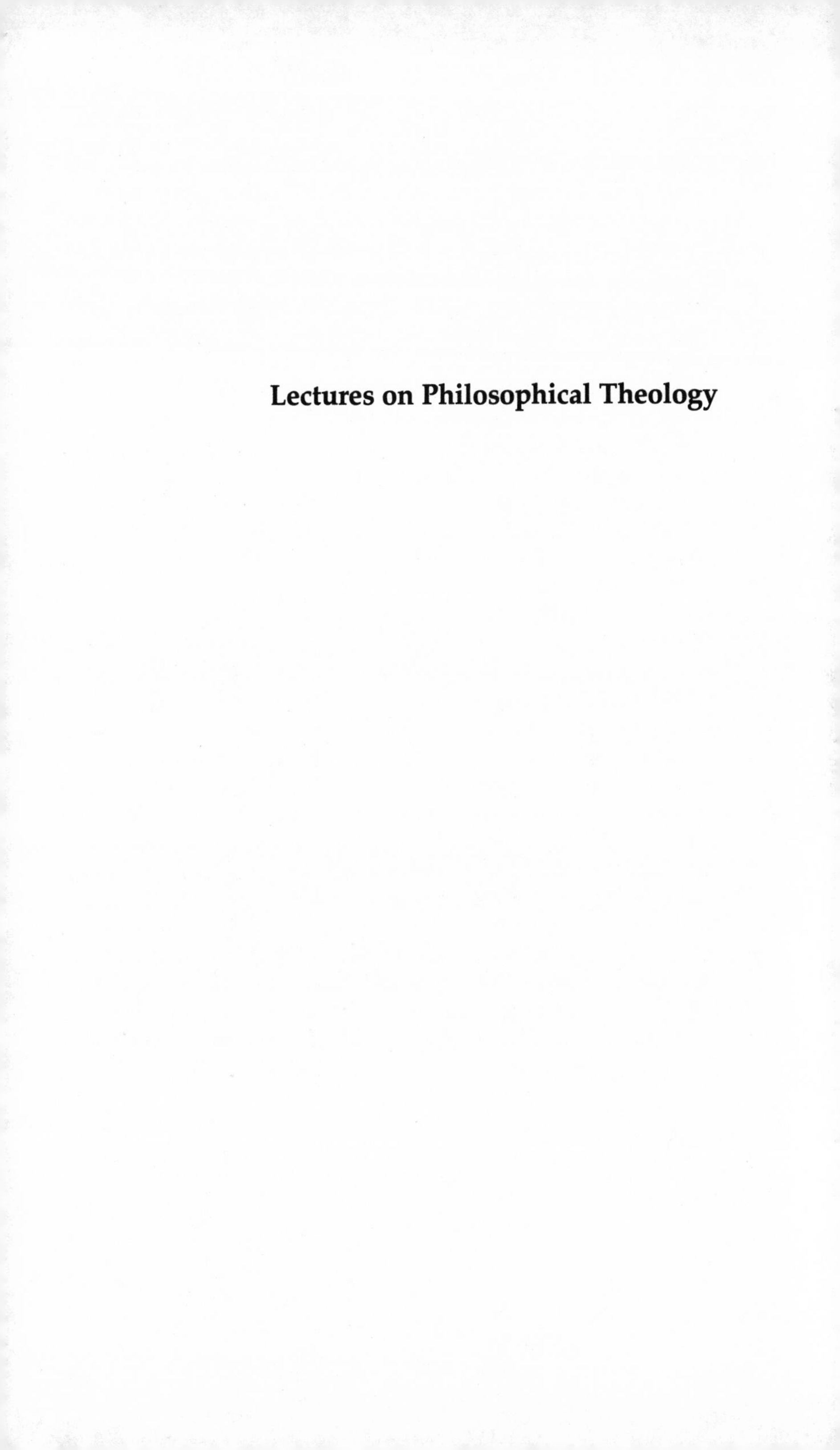

Lectures on Philosophical Theology

Introduction

[The Idea of God]

Human reason has need of an idea of highest perfection, to serve it as a standard according to which it can make determinations. As regards human affection, for example, we think of the idea of highest friendship in order to be able to determine the extent to which this or that degree of friendship approaches or falls short of it. A person can render a friendly service to someone else but still take his own welfare into consideration, or he can offer up everything to his friend with no consideration for his own advantage. The latter comes closest to the idea of perfect friendship. A concept of this kind, which is needed as a standard of lesser or greater degrees in this or that case irrespective of its own reality, is called an *idea*. But are not these ideas (such as Plato's idea of a republic, for example) all mere phantoms of the brain? By no means. For I can arrange this or that situation according to my idea. A ruler, for instance, can arrange his state according to the idea of a most perfect republic, in order to bring his state nearer to perfection.

For any idea of this kind, three elements are required: (1) completeness in the determination of the subject with respect to all its predicates (for instance, in the concept of God all realities are met with); (2) completeness in the derivation of the existence of things (for instance, the concept of a highest being which cannot be derived from any other, but which is rather that from which everything else must be derived); (3) completeness of community, or the thorough determination of community and connection of the whole.

The world depends on a supreme being, but the things in the world all mutually depend on one another. Taken together, they constitute a complete whole. The understanding always seeks to form a unity in all things, and to proceed to the maximum. Thus for instance we think of heaven as the highest degree of morality combined with the highest degree of blessedness, and of hell as the highest degree of evil combined with the greatest degree of misery. When we think of evil as the *highest degree* of evil, we think of it as an immediate inclination to take satisfaction in evil merely *because it is evil*, with neither remorse nor enticement and with no consideration for profit or advantage. We form this idea in order to determine the intermediate degrees of evil according to it.

How does an idea of reason differ from an ideal of imagination? An idea is a universal rule *in abstracto*, whereas an ideal is an individual case which I bring under this rule. Thus for example, Rousseau's Emile and the education to be given him is a true idea of reason. But nothing determinate can be said about the ideal. A person can have every excellent attribute applied to him regarding the way in which he should conduct himself as ruler, father, or friend, but this will not exhaust the account of what these attributes amount to in this or that case (an example of this is Xenophon's *Cyropaedia*.)[1] The cause of this demand for completeness lies in the fact that otherwise we could have no concept of perfection. Human virtue is always imperfect. For this reason we must have a standard, in order to see how far this imperfection falls short of the highest degree of virtue. It is the same with vice. We leave out of the idea of vice everything which could limit the degree of vice. In morality it is necessary to represent the laws in their moral perfection and purity. But it would be something else again for someone to realize such an idea. And even if this is not completely possible, the idea is still

1. The point of this illustration is a bit clearer in the Danzig manuscript of the lectures: "The idea in an *individuo* is an ideal. E.g., the Cyrus of Xenophon is an idea of a perfect prince, which Xenophon here sets forth *in concreto*" (Kant, *Gesammelte Schriften*, vol. 28, 2, 2, p. 1233).

of great utility. In his *Emile,* Rousseau himself admits that a whole lifetime (or the better part of it) would be required to give one single individual the education he describes.

Now we come to the idea of a highest being. Let us represent to ourselves: (1) A being which *excludes every deficiency*. (If, for example, we imagine a man who is at once learned and virtuous, this may be a great degree of perfection, but many deficiencies still remain.) (2) A being which contains all realities in itself. Only in this way will the concept be precisely determined. This concept can also be thought as the most perfect nature, or the combination of everything belonging to a most perfect nature (for example, understanding and will). (3) It can be considered as the highest good, to which wisdom and morality belong. The first of these perfections is called transcendental perfection; the second is called physical, and the third, practical perfection.

[What Is Theology?]

What is theology? It is the system of our knowledge of the highest being. How is ordinary knowledge distinguished from theology? Ordinary knowledge is an aggregate, in which one thing is placed next to another without regard for combination and unity. In a system, the idea of the whole rules throughout. The system of knowledge of God does not refer to the sum total of all possible knowledge of God, but only to what human reason meets with in God. The knowledge of everything in God is what we call *theologia archetypa*, and this knowledge is only to be found in God himself. The system of knowledge of that part of God which lies in human nature is called *theologia ectypa*, and it can be very deficient. It does constitute a system, however, since all the insights which reason affords us can always be thought in a unity.

The sum total of all possible knowledge of God is not possible for a human being, not even through a true revelation. But it is one of the worthiest of inquiries to see how far our reason can go in the knowledge of God. Rational theology can also be brought to completion, in the sense that no human reason has the capacity to achieve a more extensive knowledge or insight. Hence it is an advantage for reason to be able to point out its boundaries completely. In this way theology relates to the capacity for all possible knowledge of God.

All our knowledge is of two kinds, positive and negative. Positive knowledge is very limited, but this makes the gain of negative knowledge so much the greater. As regards positive knowledge of God, our knowledge is no greater than ordinary knowledge. But our negative knowledge is greater. Common practice does not see the sources from which it creates knowledge. It is thus uncertain whether there are more sources from which more knowledge could be created. This follows from the fact that common practice is not acquainted with the boundaries of its understanding.

What interest does reason have in this knowledge? Not a speculative, but a practical one. The object is much too sublime for us to be able to speculate about it. In fact, we can be led into error by speculation. But our morality has need of the idea of God to give it emphasis. Thus it should not make us more learned, but better, wiser, and more upright. For if there is a supreme being who can and will make us happy, and if there is another life, then our moral dispositions will thereby receive more strength and nourishment, and our moral conduct will be made firmer. Our reason does find a small speculative interest in these matters, but it is of very little value in comparison with the practical one. This speculative interest is only that our reason always needs a highest in order to measure and determine the less high according to it.

We sometimes ascribe an *understanding* to God. To what extent can we do this? If we do not know the boundaries of our own understanding, then even less can we think of the divine understanding. But here too we must have a maximum, and we can only obtain it by canceling all limitations. Hence we say that our understanding can only know things by means of universal characteristics, but, since this is a limitation of the human understanding, it cannot be found in God. Thus we think of a maximum understanding, that is, an intuitive understanding. This gives us no concept at all, but such a maximum serves to make the lesser degrees determinate. If for example we want to determine human benevolence, we can only do it by thinking of the highest benevolence, which is found in God. And then it is easy to determine the intermediate degrees according to it. Thus in our knowledge the concept of God is not so much extended as determined. For the maximum always has to be determinate. For instance, the concept of a right is wholly and precisely determined. But the concept of equity is quite indeterminate. For it means that I should forego my right to some extent. But how much? If I forego too much, I will violate my own right.

Hence in morality too we are referred to God. For it tells us to aspire to the highest idea of morality formed according to the highest being. But how can we do this? To this end we must see to what extent our morality falls short of the morality of the highest being. In this way the concept of God can be of service to us, and it can also serve as a gauge by which we are able to determine smaller distinctions in morals. Thus we do have a speculative interest here too. But how insignificant it is! For it is no more than a means enabling us to represent in a determinate way whatever is to be found between the maximum and nothing. How small, then, this speculative interest is compared to the practical interest which has to do with our making ourselves into better men, with uplifting our concepts of morality and with placing before our eyes the concepts of our moral conduct!

Theology cannot serve to explain the appearances of nature to us. In general it is not a correct use of reason to posit God as the ground of everything whose explanation is not evident to us. On the contrary, we must first gain insight into the laws of nature if we are to know and explain its operations. In general it is no use of reason and no explanation to say that something is due to God's omnipotence. This is a lazy reason, and we will have more to say about it later.[2] But if we ask who has so firmly established the laws of nature and who has limited its operations, then we will come to God as the supreme cause of the entirety of reason and nature. Let us now ask further: What worth has our knowledge of God, or our rational theology? It has no worth just because it deals with the highest object, or has

2. This is the error of *ignava ratio* which Kant criticizes in the *Critique of Pure Reason*, A689/B717. See also the present Lectures, opening paragraph of the Second Part.

God as its object. We ought rather to ask whether we have knowledge of this object which is appropriate to the worth of this object itself. In morality we see that not only does the object have worth, but the knowledge of it has worth too. Hence it is obvious that theology has no cause to boast just because the object of its knowledge is a being of highest worthiness. In any case our knowledge is only a shadow in comparison with the greatness of God, and our powers are far transcended by him. The real question is: Does our knowledge have worth despite this? And the answer is: Yes, insofar as it is related to religion. For religion is nothing but the application of theology to morality, that is, to a good disposition and a course of conduct well-pleasing to the highest being. *Natural religion* is thus the substratum of all religion, and the firmest support of all moral principles. And to the extent that it is the hypothesis for all religion, and gives weight to all our concepts of virtue and uprightness, natural theology contains a value which raises it above any speculation.

Are there divines[3] in natural theology? There is no such thing as being naturally learned. In revealed religion there can be a place for learning, since it must be known. But in natural religion there is no place for learning. For here there is nothing to be done but to prevent errors from creeping in, and this is fundamentally not a kind of learning. In general no knowledge of reason a priori can be called learning. Learning is the sum total of knowledge which must be taught.

The theologian or divine must have true learning, since he must interpret the Bible, and interpretation depends on languages and much else which can be taught. In the time of the Greeks, philosophical schools were divided into *physicas* and

3. Divine = *Gottesgelehrte* (literally, "one learned of God"). Kant's discussion is clearly intended as a criticism of Eberhard's use of the term *Gottesgelehrtheit*: "[In theology] the knowledge of God has to be taken in the greatest perfection possible for men; that is, it must be the richest, most correct, clearest, most evident, and most living knowledge, or, in short, it must be most scientific or learned. Such knowledge, even the more limited ones, contain *religion*. We do well to distinguish these two kinds of knowledge of God. For every man has to have religion, but not every man needs to be a divine (*Gottesgelehrte*)" (Eberhard, *Vorbereitung zur natürlichen Theologie* [Halle, 1781], p. 4).

theologicas. But the latter must not be understood to be schools studying the contemporary religious usages and learning their sacred formulas and other such superstitious stuff. Rather they were rational inquirers. They saw which concepts of God lay in reason, how far reason could proceed in the knowledge of God, where the boundaries in the field of knowledge were, and so on. This depended only on the use of reason. But knowledge of God depended on learning.

Now let us ask: What is the minimum of theology required for religion? What is the smallest knowledge of God necessary to move us to have faith in God and thus direct our course of life? What is the smallest, narrowest concept of theology? It consists only in needing a religion and having a concept of God sufficient for natural religion. But this minimum is supplied if I see that my concept of God is *possible* and that it does not contradict the laws of the understanding. Can everyone be convinced of this much? Yes, everyone can, because no one is in a position to rob us of this concept and prove it impossible. Hence this is the smallest possible requirement for religion. With only this as its basis, there is still a place for religion. But the possibility of the concept of God is supported by morality, since otherwise morality would have no incentives. Moreover, the mere possibility of such a being is sufficient to produce religion in man. But this is not the maximum of theology. It would be better if I knew that such a being actually exists. It is believed that the Greeks and Romans of antiquity who devoted themselves to an upright life had no concept of God other than the possibility of this concept. And this was sufficient to move them to a religion.

We now have sufficient insight to tell that we will be satisfied from a practical standpoint, but from a speculative standpoint our reason will find little satisfaction. As we strive to present the concept of God we will guard ourselves from errors and contradictions from a speculative standpoint, and we must hold our reason very much in check if we are to be safe from the assaults of the foes of theology. But if our aim is moral, we must first of all guard ourselves against any errors which might have an influence on our morality.

Natural theology is of two kinds (a) *theologia rationalis* and (b) *theologia empirica*. But since God is not an object of sense and hence cannot be an object of experience, we can only be capable of a *theologia empirica* through the help of a divine revelation. But from this it follows that there are no kinds of theology but those of *reason* and *revelation*. Rational theology is either *speculative* (with theoretical science as its ground) or *moral* (with practical knowledge as its object). The former could also be called *speculative theology* and the latter, which we draw from practical principles, would then be called *moral theology*. Speculative theology would further be either (1) *transcendental*, taking its origin merely from pure understanding and reason independent of all experience, or (2) *natural*. The former is to be distinguished from natural theology because in it we are able to represent God in comparison with ourselves wherever there is something in us founded on a nature from which we can draw attributes applicable to God. But in natural theology there is never the purity of concepts found in transcendental theology, where all concepts are taken from pure reason alone.

Nature is the sum total of objects of experience. I can consider nature either as the nature of the world in general or as the constitution of everything present. Hence natural theology can be of two kinds: (1) *cosmotheology*, in which I consider the nature of a world in general and argue from it to the existence of an author of the world; or (2) *physicotheology*, in which I come to know a God from the constitution of the present world.

The above is a division wholly according to logical rules. But to be precise, we should divide rational theology into (a) *transcendentalem*, (b) *naturalem*, and (c) *moralem*. In the first I think of God solely in terms of transcendental concepts. In the second I think of him in terms of physical concepts, and in the last I think of God in terms of concepts drawn from morals. If we determine this more closely, we will think of God as the original being which is (1) not a *derivativum*, not a being determined by or dependent on another, and (2) the cause of all possible and existing beings. Hence I will think of God in the following ways.

(1) I will think of him as the *ens originarium* [original being], as the *ens summum* [highest being] when I compare him with all

things in general and consider him as the highest of all beings and the root of all possible things. The concept of an *entis originarii* as an *ens summum* belongs to transcendental philosophy. This transcendental concept, in fact, is the foundation of transcendental philosophy and there is a special theology in which I think of the original being as the *ens originarium* to which belongs the properties [1] of not deriving from any other thing and [2] of being the root of everything.

(2) I will think of the *ens originarium* as the *summa intelligentia* [highest intelligence], that is, the highest being considered as the highest rational being. Whoever thinks of God merely as the *ens summum* leaves indefinite how this being is constituted. But if God is thought of as the *summa intelligentia*, he is thought of as a living being, a *living* God who has knowledge and free will. He is then thought of not as the cause of the world, but as the *author* of the world, who had to apply understanding to the production of a world and who also has free will. These first two points are in *theologia rationalis*.

(3) Finally there is the representation of the *entis originarii* as the *summum bonum*, as the *highest good*. This means that God must not only be thought of as the highest power of knowledge, but also as the highest ground of knowledge, as a system of all ends. And this theology is *theologia moralis*.

In transcendental theology we represent God as the *cause* of the world. In the theology of nature we represent him as the *author* of the world, as a living God and as a free being who has given the world its existence out of his own free power of choice, without any compulsion whatever. And finally in moral theology we represent God as the *ruler* of the world. For he could have produced something out of his free power of choice without having set any further end before himself. But in moral theology we think of God as the lawgiver of the world in relation to moral laws.

[Some Theological Terms]

Whoever assumes no theology at all is an *atheist*. Whoever assumes only transcendental theology is a *deist*. The deist will certainly concede that there is a cause of the world, but he leaves it indefinite whether this cause is a freely acting being. In transcendental theology we can even apply ontological predicates to God, and say for instance that he has realities. But whoever assumes a *theologiam naturalem* is a *theist*. The terms deist and theist are nearly indistinguishable except that the former is of latin origin and the latter is of greek origin. But this difference has been taken as the sign distinguishing two species. *Theism* consists in believing not merely in a God, but in a *living* God who has produced the world through knowledge and by means of his free will. It can now be seen that *theologia transcendentalis* is set up from pure reason alone, wholly pure of any mixture of experience. But this is not the case with *natural* theology. In it some kinds of experience must be mixed in, since I must have an example such as an intelligence (for instance, the human power of understanding, from which I infer the highest understanding). But transcendental theology represents God to me wholly separate from any experience. For how could experience teach me something universal? In transcendental theology I think of God as having no limitation. Thus I extend my concept to the highest degree and regard God as a being infinitely removed from myself. But do I become acquainted with God at all in this way?

Hence the deist's concept of God is wholly idle and useless and makes no impression on me if I assume it alone. But if transcendental theology is used as a propaedeutic or introduction to the other two kinds of theology, it is of very great and wholly excellent utility. For in transcendental theology we think of God in a wholly pure way; and this prevents anthropomorphisms from creeping into the other two kinds of theology. Hence transcendental theology is of the greatest negative utility in that it keeps us safe from errors.

But what are we to call the kind of theology in which God is thought of as the *summum bonum*, as the highest moral good? Up until now it has not been correctly distinguished and so no name has been thought up for it. It can be called *theismus moralis*, since in it God is thought of as the author of our moral laws. And this is the real theology which serves as the foundation of religion. For if I were to think of God as the author of the world but not at the same time as the ruler of the world, this would have no influence at all on my conduct. In moral theology I do not think of God as the supreme principle in the kingdom of nature, but rather as the supreme principle in the *kingdom of ends*.

But *moral theology* is something wholly different from *theological morality*, a morality in which the concept of obligation presupposes the concept of God. Such a theological morality has no principle, or if it does have one, this principle is nothing but the fact that the will of God has been revealed and discovered. But morality must not be founded on theology. It must have in itself the principle which is to be the ground of our good conduct. Afterward it can be combined with theology, and then our morality will obtain more incentives and a morally moving power. In theological morality the concept of God must determine our duties. But this is just the opposite of morality. For men picture all sorts of terrible and frightening attributes as part of their concept of God. Now of course such pictures can beget fear in us and move us to follow moral laws from compulsion or through fear of punishment. But they do not make the object interesting. For we no longer see how abominable our actions are; we abstain from them only from fear of punishment. Natural morality must be so constituted that it can be thought independently of any concept of God, and elicit our most zealous devotion solely on account of its own inner worth and excellence. But it serves to increase our devotion if after we have taken an interest in morals itself, to take interest also in the existence of God, a being who can reward our good conduct. And then we will obtain strong incentives which will determine us to the observance of moral laws. This is a highly necessary hypothesis.

Speculative theology can be divided into: (1) *ontotheology*,[4] (2) *cosmotheology*, and (3) *physicotheology*. The first considers God merely in terms of concepts (and it is just *theologia transcendentalis*, which considers God as the principle of all possibility). Cosmotheology presupposes something existing and infers a highest being from the existence of a world in general. And finally, physicotheology makes use of experience of the present

4. Pölitz's text reads *Ontologie*.

world in general and infers from this to the existence of an author of the world and to the attributes which would belong to its author as such.

Anselm was the first to try to establish the necessity of a highest being from mere concepts, proceeding from the concept of an *entis realissimi*. Even if this theology is of no great utility from a practical standpoint, it still has the advantage of purifying our concepts and cleansing them of everything which we as human beings belonging to the world of sense might ascribe to the abstract concept of God. It is the ground of every possible theology.

Cosmotheology has been treated most notably by Leibniz and Wolff. In this kind of theology it is presupposed that there exists some object of experience and then the attempt is made to establish the existence of a highest being from this pure experience. Wolff doubted that the existence of a being containing the ground of all possibility could be proven merely from the concept of such a being. So he said: Something exists. Now it must either exist for itself or have a cause as the ground of its existence. The first cause must be the being of all beings. Hence we see that cosmotheology is just as abstract as ontotheology, for it does not help me much to be told that something exists which either exists for itself or has another cause as the ground of its existence. And if we investigate whether this cause contains every perfection in itself, the result is the concept that there must be a being of all beings, an original being which depends on nothing else.

All the world aims at popularity and tries to provide insight into concepts by means of easily grasped examples. So there is good cause to seek an intuitive grasp even of the highest concept. But in order to keep a sure foothold as well and not to wander in labyrinths outside the field of experience, it is also demanded with right that the absolute idea be represented *in concreto*. This is why we come to physicotheology. It has been treated by many, and it was already the foundation of the teachings of Anaxagoras and Socrates. Physicotheology has the utility of presenting the highest being as the highest intelligence and as the author of purposiveness, order, and beauty. It is adapted to the whole human race, for it can enlighten and give an intuitive appeal to our concepts of God. But it must also be remarked that physicotheology cannot have any *determinate* concept of God. For only reason can represent completeness and totality. In physicotheology I see God's power. But can I say determinately, this is *omnipotence* or the highest degree of power? Hence I cannot infer a perfection of the highest kind.

The Ontological Proof

This proof gives me ontotheology, in which I can think of the highest perfection as determined in all its predicates. But the judgments our reason makes about things are either affirmative or negative. That is, when I predicate something of a thing, this predicate I apply to the thing expresses either that something is (or is met with) in the thing, or else that something is not in it. A predicate which expresses being in a thing contains a *reality;* but one which expresses nonbeing contains its negation. Every negation presupposes some reality. Therefore I cannot know any negation unless I know the reality opposed to it. For how could I perceive a mere deficiency without being acquainted with what is lacking?

Every thing in the world has realities and negations in it. Something composed only of negations and lacking in everything would be a nothing, a nonentity. Hence every thing, if it is to be a thing at all, must have some realities. Every thing in the world also has some negations, and it is just this relation between realities and negations which constitutes the distinction between things. But we find some negations in things whose corresponding realities can never be met with in the world. How are these negations possible, if they are nothing but limitations on reality? Or how can we judge the magnitude of reality in these things and determine the degree of their perfection? Since according to the principles of its own nature reason can only infer the particular from the universal in making judgments about the degree of reality in things, it must think of some maximum of reality from which it can proceed and according to which it can measure all other things. A thing of this kind, in which all realities are contained, would be the only complete thing, because it is perfectly determined in regard to all possible predicates. And just for this reason such an *ens realissimum* [most real being] would also be the ground of the possibility of all other things. For I could think of the possibility of infinitely many things merely by thinking of the highest reality as limited in infinitely many ways. If I retain some realities but limit them and wholly leave out other realities, then I have a thing which has both realities and negations, and whose limitations presuppose some greater reality. For instance, we can think of a certain light, and also think of infinite modifications of it by mixing shadow with the light. In this case the light would be the reality, and shadow the negation. Now I can think of much light and little shadow or little light and much shadow, and whatever I think of in each case according to the measuring rules of more and less would be the aspects and modifications of the light.

This same principle accounts for copper engraving and etching. Just as in these arts the light contains the ground of the possibility of all the modifications arising from it, so in the same way the *ens realissimum* contains the ground of the possibility of all other things when I limit it so that negations arise. This pure concept of the understanding, the concept of God as a thing having every reality, is to be found in every human understanding. But it is often expressed in other formulas.

But is the object of this concept also actual? That is another question. In order to prove the existence of such a being, Descartes argued that a being containing every reality in itself must *necessarily* exist, since existence is also a reality. If I think of an *ens realissimum* I must also think of this reality along with it. In this way he derived the necessary existence of such a being merely out of a pure concept of the understanding. And this would certainly have been a splendid thing, if only his proof had been correct. For then my own reason would compel me to assume the existence of such a being, and I would have to give up my own reason if I wanted to deny its existence. Further, I could then prove incontrovertibly that there could be only one such being. For I could not think of more than one being which includes everything real in itself. If there were several such beings, then either they would not be *realissima*, or else they would have to be one and the same being.

The Cosmological Proof

In this proof I presuppose that something exists (hence I presuppose an experience), and thus the proof built on this presupposition is no longer derived from pure reason as was the transcendental proof already discussed. But the experience with which I begin is the simplest experience I could possibly presuppose. It is just the experience that I am. Then, along with Leibniz and Wolff, I argue as follows: I am either necessary or contingent. But the changes which go on in me show that I am not necessary. Therefore I am contingent. But if I am contingent, there must be somewhere external to me a ground for my existence, which is the reason why I am as I am and not otherwise. This ground of my existence must be absolutely necessary. For if it too were contingent, then it could not be the ground of my existence, since it would once again have need of something else containing the ground of its existence. This absolutely necessary being, however, must contain in itself the ground of its own existence, and consequently the ground of the existence of the whole world. For the whole world is contingent, and hence it cannot contain in itself the reason why it is as it is and not otherwise. But a being which contained in itself the ground of the existence of all things would also have to contain in itself the ground of its *own* existence. For there is nothing from which it could be derived. And this being is *God*. Then Wolff went on to infer the highest perfection of such a being from its absolute necessity.

Except for what pertains to its primary source, this cosmological proof is fundamentally just as abstract as the transcendental one. For this source is empirical, but beyond it we have to do here too only with pure concepts. It is easy to see that in the cosmological proof the transcendental proof is presupposed as correct and gives the cosmological proof all its strength. On the other hand, if the earlier proof is incorrect, this second proof breaks down of itself. For it is only if I can prove that a most perfect being must necessarily exist that I can conclude conversely that an absolutely necessary being must be a most perfect being.

The Physicotheological Proof

The physicotheological proof is the one in which we infer from the constitution of the present world to the nature of its author. This proof is nearly identical with the cosmological one. The only difference is that in the cosmological proof the concept of an author of the world is abstracted from the concept of a world in general, whereas in the physicotheological proof it is abstracted from the *present* world. The source of this proof is wholly empirical and the proof itself very popular and appealing, whereas the ontological and cosmological proofs are rather dry and abstract.

It is now time to introduce a correction relating to the systematic application of the proofs for God's existence. This correction is necessary because we have not expressed the matter precisely enough above. It consists in pointing out that the ontological and cosmological proofs both belong to transcendental theology because both of them are derived from *principiis a priori*.[5] This has already been made sufficiently clear as regards the ontological proof. But it might appear as if the cosmological proof were borrowed from experience, as we have even asserted above. But on closer inspection we will find that no experience of a world really need be presupposed. Rather, the existence of a world may merely be assumed as a hypothesis. Then I argue as follows: If there is a world, it must be either contingent or necessary, etc. And not: There exists a world, etc. Thus in this inference I need no experience of the world at all, or of the manner in which it is constituted. Instead I make use of the mere concept of a world, be it the best or the worst world, as you like. Thus the whole cosmological proof is built on pure concepts of understanding and to this extent it belongs to transcendental theology, which argues from *principiis a priori*. But the physico-

5. Following Eberhard, Kant first classified the Leibnizian proof *a contingentia mundi* as an a posteriori proof. His own opinion, however, is that it is just as much an a priori proof as the ontological proof is. (Cf. Eberhard, *Vorbereitung*, p. 28.)

theological proof is derived wholly from empirical principles, because I use my actual perception of the existing world as its foundation. But if transcendental theology does not succeed, physicotheology will not succeed either. For physicotheology can never give a determinate concept of God without transcendental theology, and an indeterminate concept is no help at all. The precise concept of God is the concept of a most perfect thing. But I can never derive such a concept from experience, for the highest perfection can never be given me in any possible experience. For example, I could never prove God's omnipotence through experience, even if I assume a million suns surrounded with a million universes in an immeasurably immense space, with each of these universes occupied by both rational and irrational creatures. For a great power could have produced even a hundred million and a thousand million suns. From any *factum* I could only infer a great power, an immeasurable power. But what is meant by an *immeasurable* power? Only a power such that my power is so small compared to it that I have no capacity to measure it. But this is still not omnipotence.

Likewise, even though I may wonder at the magnitude, order, and chainlike combination of all things in the world, I cannot conclude that only one being has produced it. There could just as easily have been several powerful beings, each taking pleasure in working his own field.[6] Or at least I cannot refute this supposition from my experience of the world. This is why the ancients, who founded their proofs for God on what they experienced of the world, produced such contradictory results. Anaxagoras, and later Socrates, believed in one God. Epicurus believed in none, or believed that if there is one, he has nothing to do with the world. Others believed in many gods or in supreme principles of good and evil. This happened because each considered the world from a different point of view. One saw an

6. At this point Kant may have in mind the following passage from Hume: "And what shadow of an argument, continued Philo, can you produce, from your hypothesis, to prove the unity of the Deity? A great number of men join in building a house or ship, in rearing a city, in framing a commonwealth: why may not several deities combine in contriving and framing a world? This is only so much greater similarity to human affairs" (Hume, *Dialogues concerning Natural Religion*, Part V [New York, 1948], p. 39).

order of the highest harmony derived from an infinite understanding. The other perceived everything only according to the physical laws of coming to be and perishing. Yet another remarked on the wholly contradictory purposes, for instance, earthquakes, fiery volcanoes, furious hurricanes, and the destruction of everything which was so excellently set up.

The abstraction of concepts of God from these empirically founded perceptions can beget nothing but contradictory systems. Our experience of the world is too limited to permit us to infer a highest reality from it. Before we could argue that the present world is the most perfect of all possible ones and prove from this that its author is of the highest perfection, we would first have to know the whole totality of the world, every means and every end reached by it. The natural theologians have certainly seen this. So they follow their proof only to the point where they believe it has been thoroughly established that there exists a *prima causa mundi* [first cause of the world], and then by a leap they fall into transcendental theology and prove from it that the *prima causa mundi* (the *ens originarium*) would have to be absolutely necessary, and hence an *ens realissimum* as well. From this we see that physicotheology rests wholly on transcendental theology. If transcendental theology is correct and well-founded, physicotheology does an excellent service, and all the objections against the highest perfection based on the conflicts in nature will collapse of themselves. For then we already know to the point of complete conviction that the *ens originarium* is an *ens realissimum*, and consequently we know that everywhere he must have left the imprint of his highest perfection. And we know that it can only be due to our limitation and shortsightedness if we do not see the best everywhere, because we are not in a position to survey the whole and its future consequences from which the greatest and most perfect result would certainly have to arise.

There are no speculative proofs for the existence of God except these three. There is the ancients' concept of the *primo motore* [first mover] and the necessity of its existence on account of the fact that it is impossible for matter to have moved itself first. But this proof is already contained in the cosmological proof. And in fact it is not even as general, since the cosmological proof is founded on the thought of change and contingency, and not merely on the motion of the corporeal world. But if anyone tried to prove the existence of God from the agreement of all peoples in believing in him, a proof of this kind would not work at all. For history and experience teach us just as well that all peoples have believed in ghosts and witches too, and still believe in them.[7]

Thus all speculation depends, in substance, on the transcendental concept. But if we posit that it is not correct, would we then have to give up the knowledge of God? Not at all. For then we would only lack the scientific knowledge that God exists. But a great field would still remain to us, and this would be the belief or faith[8] that God exists. This faith we will derive a priori from *moral principles*. Hence if in what follows we raise doubts about these speculative proofs and take issue with the supposed demonstrations of God's existence, we will not thereby undermine faith in God. Rather, we will clear the road for practical proofs. We are merely throwing out the false presumptions of human reason when it tries from itself to demonstrate the existence of God with apodictic certainty. But from moral principles we will assume a faith in God as the principle of every religion.

Atheism (that is, godlessness or denial of God), can be either *skeptical* or *dogmatic*. The former disputes only the proofs for the existence of a God and especially their apodictic certainty, but not God's existence itself, or at least its possibility. Hence a skeptical atheist can still have religion, because he sincerely admits that it is even more impossible to prove that God does

7. Eberhard agrees with Kant in dismissing the argument from the agreement of peoples: "The proof of God's existence drawn from the agreement of peoples has too many difficulties to be used with certainty. For (1) it gets involved in historical investigations pertaining to the minor premise, and (2) the major premise will also be disputed, because the knowledge of God in many peoples is mixed with errors and superstition" (Eberhard, *Vorbereitung*, p. 60). (Eberhard probably takes the argument to go something like this: *Major premise*: Whatever all peoples agree on is true. *Minor premise*: All peoples agree that God exists. *Therefore*, God exists.)

8. *Glaube* means either simply "belief" or (in religious contexts) "faith." It will be translated below in whichever way seems most appropriate to the context, and no other word will be translated either as "belief" or as "faith."

not exist than to prove that he does. He denies only that human reason could ever prove of God's existence with certainty through speculation. But, on the other hand, he sees with equal certainty that it can never establish that God does not exist. Now the belief in a merely possible God as ruler of the world is obviously the minimum of theology. But it is of great enough influence that it can give rise to morality in any man who already knows the necessity of his duties with apodictic certainty. It is wholly different with the atheist who straightway denies the existence of a God, and who declares in general that it is impossible for there to be a God. Either there haver never been such dogmatic atheists, or else they were the worst of men, for in them all the incentives of morality have broken down. And it is the atheist of this kind who is to be contrasted with moral theism.

Moral Theism

Moral theism is, of course, critical, since it follows all the speculative proofs for God's existence step by step and knows them to be insufficient. Indeed, the moral theist asserts without qualification that it is impossible for speculative reason to demonstrate the existence of such a being with apodictic certainty. But he is nevertheless firmly convinced of the existence of this being, and he has a faith beyond all doubt from practical grounds. The foundation on which he builds his faith is unshakeable, and it can never be overthrown, not even if all mankind united to undermine it. It is a fortress in which the moral man can find refuge with no fear of ever being driven from it, because every attack on it will come to nothing. Hence a faith in God built on this foundation is as certain as a mathematical demonstration. The foundation of faith is morality, the whole system of duties, which is known a priori with apodictic certainty through pure reason. This absolutely necessary morality of actions flows from the idea of a freely acting rational being and from the nature of action itself. Hence nothing firmer or more certain can be thought in any science than our obligation to moral actions. Reason would have to cease to be if it could deny this obligation in any way. For moral actions do not depend on their consequences or circumstances. They are determined for men once and for all simply through their own nature. It is only through making it his purpose to do his duty that anyone becomes a human being, and otherwise he is either a beast or a monster. His own reason bears witness against him when he so forgets himself as to act contrary to duty and makes him despicable and abominable in his own eyes. But if he is conscious of following his duty, then a man is certain of being a member or link in the chain of the kingdom of all ends. This thought gives him comfort and reassurance. It makes him inwardly noble and worthy of happiness. And it raises him to the hope that he may constitute a whole together with all other rational beings in the kingdom of morals, in just the same way that everything is connected and unified in the kingdom of nature. Now man has a secure foundation on which to build his faith in God. For although his virtue must be without any selfishness, after denying the many claims of seductive temptations he may still feel in himself the impulse to hope for a lasting happiness. He tries to act according to the duties he finds grounded in his own nature. But he also has senses which oppose these duties with their continuous dazzle, and he would in the end be blinded by this dazzle if he had no further incentives and powers to help him withstand it. Hence in order that he might not set against his own powers, his reason compels him to think of a being whose will is those very commands which he knows to be given for themselves a priori with apodictic certainty. He will have to think of this being as most perfect, for otherwise his morality could not obtain reality through it. It must be *omniscient* if it is to know even the smallest stirrings of his innermost heart and all the motives and intentions of his actions. For this, only omniscience will suffice; a merely great knowledge will not be enough.

This being must also be *omnipotent* if it is to arrange the whole of nature according to the morality of my actions. It must be *holy* and *just*, for otherwise I would have no hope that the fulfillment of my duties would be well pleasing to it. From this we see that the moral theist can have a wholly precise and determinate concept of God by arranging this concept in accordance with morality. And at the same time he renders unnecessary everything that the skeptical atheist attacks. For he needs no speculative proofs of God's existence. He is convinced of it with certainty, because otherwise he would have to reject the necessary laws of morality which are grounded in the nature of his being. Thus he derives theology from morality, yet not from speculative but from practical evidence; not through knowledge, but through faith. But a necessary practical hypothesis is with regard to our practical knowledge what an axiom is with respect to speculative knowledge. Hence the existence of a wise governor of the world is a *necessary postulate of practical reason*.

First Part: Transcendental Theology

In this knowledge of God from pure concepts, we have three constitutive concepts of God, and they are the following.

(1) The concept of God as the *original being* (*ens originarium*). In this concept I think of God as a thing in general which is not derived from anything else, as the only original being which is not derivative. Thus I represent God as completely isolated from everything, as existing for himself and from himself and as standing in community with no other being. This concept of an *entis originarii* is the foundation of cosmotheology. For it is from this concept that I infer the absolute necessity and highest perfection of God.

(2) The concept of God as the *highest being* (*ens summum*). In this concept I think of God as a being having every reality. It is from this concept of an *entis realissimi* and from its attributes that I derive its originality and absolute necessity. This concept of God as an *ente maximo* [greatest being] is the foundation of ontotheology.

(3) The concept of God as the *being of all beings* (*ens entium*). In this concept I think of God not only as the original being for itself which is derived from no other, but also as the highest ground of all other things, as the being from which everything else is derived. This we can call the *all-sufficiency* of God. These three concepts of God as the original being, the highest being, and the being of all beings are the foundation of everything else.

We will of course ascribe various other predicates to God in what follows. But these three are the only special determinations of the fundamental concept of God.

First Section: Ontotheology

[The *ens realissimum*]

In ontotheology we consider God as the *highest* being, or at least we make this concept our foundation. But how will I be able to think of a highest being through pure reason, *merely as a thing*? Every thing must have something positive which expresses some being in it. A mere not-being cannot constitute any thing. The concept *de ente omni modo negativo* [of a being in every way negative] is the concept of a *non entis*. Consequently, since each thing must have reality, we can represent every possible thing either as an *ens realissimum* or as an *ens partim reale, partim negativum*. But in the case of any thing which has only some reality, something is always still lacking, and hence it is not a complete thing. A highest thing, therefore, would have to be one which has all reality. For in this case alone do I have a thing whose thorough determination is bound up with its concept, because it is thoroughly and completely determined with respect to all possible *praedicatorum oppositorum* [opposed predicates]. Consequently the concept of an *entis realissimi* is the concept of an *entis summi*. For all things except this being are *partim realia, partim negativa* and thus their concepts are not thoroughly determinate. For example, the concept of a perfect human being as human does not determine whether this human being is old or young, tall or short, learned or unlearned. Hence such things are not complete things because they do not have all reality, but are instead mixed with negations.

But what are negations? They are nothing but limitations of realities. For no negation can be thought unless the positive has been thought previously. How could I think of a mere deficiency, of darkness without a concept of light, or poverty without a concept of prosperity? Thus if every negative concept is derived in that it always presupposes a reality, then every thing in its thorough determination as an *ens partim reale, partim nega-*

tivum [a being partly real and partly negative] also presupposes an *ens realissimum* with respect to its realities and negations, because they are nothing but limitations of the highest reality. For when I wholly deny some realities which belong to an *entis realissimi*, there arise negations which give me the concept of an *entis partim realis, partim negativi* when I combine them with the remaining realities. Hence the concept of an *entis realissimi* contains simultaneously the ground for every other concept. Consequently it is the fundamental standard according to which I have to think or even judge all other things. Thus for instance I can think of something which does not know only if I have previously thought of a being who knows everything and then wholly canceled this reality.

From this it follows that the concept of an *entis realissimi* is at the same time the concept of an *entis originarii* from which all the concepts of other things are derived. But obviously this is only an *entis originarii logice talis* [a logically original being], a being whose concept cannot be derived from any other concept because all other concepts of things must be derived from it. Thus an *ens realissimum* is also an *ens logice originarium*. On the other hand, *omne ens limitatum* [every limited being] is also an *ens derivativum* [derivative being].

When Eberhard speaks of *mixed realities*, he is using an improper expression.[1] For a mixture of a reality and a negation, of something and nothing, cannot be thought. If I am to mix something with something else, I must have something actual. But negations are mere deficiencies. Hence if a thing has something negative along with what is real (for example, a darkened room, etc.) then in this case there is no mixing in of the negation, but rather a limitation of the reality. Thus in the case cited above I could not mix the negation darkness in with the light as something real. Rather, the negative darkness arose when I reduced and limited the reality light. But the *logical* mixture of concepts is something wholly different. Here I can cer-

1. "Realities are either pure or mixed. . . . The latter are realities which include negations in themselves. . . . In this case we have to separate the negative element from our concept if we are to retain something real" (Eberhard, *Vorbereitung*, pp. 14–15). It seems clear that Eberhard's view is substantially the same as Kant's on this point. Kant's objection to the phrase "mixed reality" appears to be no more than a verbal quibble.

tainly say that the concept of a negation is mixed in with my concept of reality, for my concept of something negative is a concept every bit as much as my concept of something real is a concept. Hence here I have things which can be mixed with one another. But this is not the case with the objects themselves, it is only the case with my idea of the object.

More important than this is the proposition of those scholastic theologians who said that every attribute of God is in fact God himself. Expressed completely and precisely, the proposition is this: any single reality without limitation considered as a ground is at the same time my whole concept of God. If we examine this proposition, we find that it has an actual foundation. Every reality, if I think of it without limitation, is God himself. God is the Omniscient, the Omnipotent, the Eternal. In these cases I have only single realities without limits and I represent God wholly under each of them, because I think of each unlimited reality simultaneously as a ground from which I understand every other unlimited reality. For instance, when I represent omniscience, I regard it as a ground through which I posit omniscience, omnipotence, etc. And I infer with right that the being to which this single reality belongs without limitation is a being to which all the other realities also belong. And from this arises the concept of God. God is a necessary idea of our understanding, because he is the substratum of the possibility of all things. This point was already established above. But now the question is whether this idea of ours also has objective reality, that is, whether there actually exists a being corresponding to our idea of God. Some have wanted to prove this from the fact that in our concept there is nothing which contradicts it. Now this is obviously true, for our whole concept of God consists of realities. But it is impossible for one reality to contradict another, since a contradiction requires that something be and also not be. But this not-being would be a negation, and nothing of this kind can be thought in God. Yet the fact that there is nothing contradictory in my concept of God proves only the *logical possibility* of the concept, that is, the possibility of forming the concept in my understanding. For a self-contradictory concept is no concept at all.

But if I am to give objective reality to my concept and prove that there actually exists an object corresponding to my concept—more is surely required for this than the fact that there is nothing in my concept which contradicts itself. For how can a concept which is logically possible, merely in its logical possibility, constitute at the same time the real possibility of an object? For this, not only an analytic judgment is required, but also a synthetic one. That is, I must be able to know that the effects of the realities do not cancel one another. For instance, decisiveness and caution are both realities, but their effects are often of such a kind that one cancels the other. Now I have no capacity to judge a priori whether the realities combined in the concept of God cancel each other in their effects, and hence I cannot establish the possibility of my concept directly. But on the other hand, I may also be sure that no human being could ever prove its impossibility.

Let us now ask how we come to the concept of a maximum of all realities. The answer is this: insofar as the reality is finite, we must leave every limitation out of its concept if we want to apply it to the concept of a *realissimi*. For fundamentally we can only think of God by ascribing to him without any limitation everything real which we meet with in ourselves. But it is often very difficult to separate out every limitation, because we ourselves are limited creatures and are often unable to represent the real except under limitations. In such a case, where we are not in a position to remove all the limitations from our concept, we still do not need to give up the reality itself; rather we can say that we do ascribe it to God, only without any limitations, because in fact something real is its foundation. Thus for example it is very difficult for us to think of eternity without any limitations. But we must nevertheless have it in our concept of God, because it is a reality. So we ascribe it to God and admit the inability of our reason to think it in a wholly pure way.

As for God's understanding, we must think of it as intuitive, as opposed to our discursive understanding, which is able to form concepts of things only from universal characteristics. But this is a limitation which must be left out of the reality of understanding if I am to apply this reality to God. Hence God's understanding will not be a faculty of thinking but a faculty of intuiting.

The concept of the infinite is taken from mathematics, and belongs only to it.[2] For this concept never determines an absolute magnitude. On the contrary, it always determines only a relative one. It is the concept of a magnitude which in relation to its measure as unity is greater than any number. Hence infinity never determines how great something is. For it does not determine the standard (or unity) and a great deal depends on this in fact. For example, if I represent space as infinite, I can assume either miles or diameters of the earth as the standard or unity with respect to which it is infinite. If I assume miles as the standard, then I can say that universal space is greater than any number of miles, even if I think of centillions of them. But if I assume diameters of the earth as my standard, or even distances to the sun. I will still be able to say here that universal space is greater than any number, in this case, of diameters of the earth and distances to the sun, even if I think of centillions of them. But who does not see that in the last case the infinity is greater than in the first, because here the unity with respect to which universal space is greater than any number is much greater than it was before? But from this we also see that the concept of infinity only expresses a relation to our incapacity to determine the concept of magnitude, because the magnitude in question is greater than every number I can think of, and hence gives me no determinate concept of the magnitude itself. Thus when I call an object infinite the only advantage this gives me is that I gain an insight into my inability to express the magnitude of this object in numbers. I may be very impressed and astonished at the object in this way, but on the other hand, I can never come

2. Eberhard (*Vorbereitung*, pp. 15–17) claims that God is both mathematically (indeterminately) infinite and metaphysically (determinately) infinite. In the following two paragraphs, Kant subjects these claims to criticism. His objection to calling God "mathematically infinite" was in fact derived from Leibniz. But Eberhard's notion of "metaphysical infinity" would seem to be nothing but the traditional rationalist conception of a "reality" or "perfection," to which Kant wholeheartedly subscribed. And in fact Kant himself continues to call God "infinite" in this sense.

to know the absolute magnitude of the object by means of it. Thus the concept of infinity can have a great deal of aesthetic beauty on account of its ability to move me deeply. But it does not help me at all to say with precision how great the object itself is. Moreover, if I am to assume an object to be infinite, I must always assume that it is homogeneous with something else. For instance if I call the divine understanding infinite I must assume my understanding as a standard of unity, and then admit that the magnitude of the divine understanding is greater than everything I can think of as an understanding. But this does not help me in the least to be able to say determinately *how great* the divine understanding is. Thus we see that I cannot come a single step further in my knowledge of God by applying the concept of mathematical infinity to him. For through this concept I only learn that I can never express the concept of God's greatness in numbers. But this gives me no insight into God's absolute greatness. I cannot even find any measure for it. For where is there a unity which is homogeneous with God?

Might we perhaps succeed in finding this measure by means of the concept of metaphysical infinity? But what is the meaning of "metaphysical infinity?" In this concept we understand perfections in their highest degree, or better yet, without any degree. The *omnitudo realitatis* [All of reality] is what is called metaphysical infinity. Now it is true that through this concept we do gain a precise concept of God's greatness. For this total reality does determine only his absolute greatness. But here I need no homogeneous measure, no unity to be compared with God in order to bring out his greatness relative to it. Rather, I have here a determinate concept of this greatness itself. For I see that everything which is truly a reality is to be met with in him. But the concept of totality is always wholly precise, and I can never think of it as more or less than it is. On the other hand, I cannot see why I ought to express an ontological concept (the concept of totality) in terms of mathematical infinity. Should I not use a term congruent with the concepts of this science, instead of permitting an ambiguity by usurping an expression from another science, thus running the risks of letting an alien concept creep in as well? Hence in theology we can easily dispense with the term *metaphysical infinity*. The ontological concept expressed is not suitably rendered by a term of mathematical origin, and would be better signified by the term *All of reality*. But if we want a special term for this concept, we would do better to choose the expression *all-sufficiency* (*omnisufficientia*). This expression represents everything real in God to us as a ground (*ens entium*), because *sufficientia* always expresses the relation of a ground to its consequences. We would also do better to be satisfied with the pure concept of our reason, *omnitudo realitatis*. For this concept is the fundamental measure by which I can determine the absolute greatness of God.

Above we have already firmly established the universal concept of God as an *ens realissimum*. This is the ideal our reason needs as a higher standard for what is less complete. And we have seen further that this concept of a most perfect being has to be at the same time the concept of a highest being. Now the question is: Which predicates will we ascribe to this being, and in what way must we proceed in arranging these predicates of God so that they do not contradict the concept of a being which is the most primary of all? At this point we still have to do only with mere concepts, and we are not troubling ourselves as yet with whether these concepts actually correspond to an object. We have thought of a being as the substratum of the possibility of all other beings, and now we are asking how this ideal must be constituted. Hence we want to see which predicates can agree with the concept of this highest and most perfect being. This investigation is most necessary, since otherwise the whole concept is of no help to us, and cannot in general be rightly thought by us unless we determine the predicates which are congruent to it. But this investigation will also be of great utility to us in that it teaches us to know God as far as human reason is capable of this knowledge. It gives us convenient rules as to how we are to speak of God, and what we are to say of him. And it will recommend caution and care to us, so that nothing creeps into our concept of God which is contrary to his highest reality.

What predicates, then, can be thought in an *ente realissimo*? What are its attributes? We have already seen that nothing can be predicated of the concept of an *entis realissimi* except realities.

But where will we find these realities? What are they? And how can we (and how must we) ascribe them to God? Every reality is either given me through pure reason independently of any experience, or met with by me in the world of sense. I may ascribe the first kind of reality to God without hesitation, for realities of this kind apply to things in general and determine them through pure understanding. Here no experience is involved and the realities are not even affected by sensibility. Hence if I predicate them of God I need not fear that I am confusing him with an object of sense. For in this case I am only ascribing to him what is true of him as a thing in general. It lies already in my concept of him as an *ente realissimo* that he must be a thing, and therefore I have to ascribe to him every reality which can be predicated of him as a thing. Now since these a priori realities refer to the universal attributes of a thing in general, they are called *ontological* predicates. They are purely transcendental concepts. To this class of realities belong God's possibility, his existence, his necessity, or whatever kind of existence flows from his concept; also the concept of substance, the concept of unity of substance, simplicity, infinity, duration, presence, and others as well. But all these concepts determine only the concept of a *thing in general*. They are only predicates *in abstracto* which the deist ascribes to God. It is impossible for us to be satisfied with them alone, for such a God would be of no help to us. He would be only a thing, wholly isolated and for itself, standing in no relation to us. This concept of God must certainly constitute the beginning of all our knowledge of God, but it is useless when taken only for itself, and it would be quite dispensable for us if we could not know more of God than this. If this concept of God is to be of use to us, we will have to see if these ontological predicates cannot be applied to examples *in concreto*. The theist does this when he thinks of God as the *supreme intelligence*. If we are to ascribe predicates to God *in concreto*, we will have to take the materials for the concept of God from empirical principles and empirical knowledge. But in the whole of our experience we find nothing which has more reality than *our own soul*. Its realities thus have to be taken from our knowledge of ourselves. They will be psychological predicates which can be ascribed to God along with his ontological predicates. But since all these predicates are borrowed from experience, and since in the whole of experience we meet with nothing but phenomena, at this point we must exercise great care so that we do not let ourselves be blinded by a mere show and ascribe predicates to God which can only be true of objects of sense. Hence we must note the following rules of caution:

(1) Regarding *the choice of the predicates themselves*: What kinds of predicates shall we take from experience so as to be able to unite them with the concept of God? Nothing but pure realities. But in the whole world there is no thing which has *pure* reality. Rather, every thing which can be given us through experience is a *partim reale, partim negativum*. Hence great difficulties arise at this point, because many of my concepts are associated with determinations which have some deficiency in them. But such negations cannot be ascribed to God. Hence I must first proceed *via negationis* [by the way of negation].[3] That is, I must carefully separate out everything sensible inhering in my representation of this or that reality, and leave out everything imperfect and negative. Then I must ascribe to God the pure reality which is left over. But this is extremely difficult, for often very little or nothing at all is left over after I reject the limitations. Or at least I can never think of the pure positive without the sensible element which is woven into my representation of it. In a case like this I have to say that if I do ascribe this or that *realitas phaenomenon* [phenomenal reality] to God, I do it only insofar as all limitations have been separated from it. But if the negative element cannot be separated without canceling the concept at the same time, then in this case I will not be able to predicate the concept of God at all. Thus, for instance, I cannot ascribe extension to God as a predicate, because it is only a concept of sense, and if I separate everything negative from it, nothing real at all is left over. Similarly, after I remove everything negative and sensible from the concept of matter, I retain nothing but the con-

3. Both Kant's texts speak of the *via negationis*. Cf. Eberhard, *Vorbereitung*, p. 26, and Baumgarten, *Metaphysica* (Halle, 1963), §826.

cept of an externally active power. And in the case of the concept of spatial presence, if I leave out the condition of sense (i.e. space), nothing but the pure reality of presence is left over. From these concepts, therefore, I will be able to apply to God only the realities themselves, power and presence.

In this way I will be able to determine the quality of divine predicates *via negationis*. That is, I can determine which predicates drawn from experience can be applied to my concept of God after all negations have been separated from them. But in this way I cannot come to know the quantity of the reality in God. On the contrary, the reality remaining in my concepts after all the limitations have been left out will be quite insignificant and small in degree. Hence if I meet with any reality in any of the attributes of things given to me through experience, I must ascribe this reality to God in the highest degree and with infinite significance. This is called proceeding *per viam eminentiae* [by the way of eminence].[4] But I cannot proceed in this way unless I have first brought out the pure reality *via negationis*. But if I have neglected this task and have not carefully separated everything negative from my concept, then my concept of God will be wholly corrupt if I predicate the concept of this reality as it is met with in appearance. It is from this that anthropomorphism arises.

Hence first the limits must be left out and only the pure reality which is left over must be ascribed to God. But it must be ascribed *via eminentiae*. For instance, not merely power, but *infinite* power must be ascribed to God, and not merely an understanding, but an *infinite* understanding. But we can never arrive fully at the attributes of God, so as to be able to know how they are constituted *in themselves*. For instance, if we take the human understanding, it is not enough to magnify it infinitely *via eminentiae*. For it would still remain a limited understanding and would grow in the quickness of its knowledge. Rather, we must first have left out all the limits inhering in it as an understanding that can only know things *discursively*. But since the pure reality

4. Cf. Eberhard, *Vorbereitung*, p. 26, and Baumgarten, *Metaphysica*, §826.

which is then left over (i.e. understanding) cannot in general be comprehended by us at all, there is only one path still left open to us.

(2) Regarding the *way of proceeding* in ascribing to God those realities abstracted from concepts of sense: This is the noble way of *analogy*. But what does this proceeding *per analogiam* consist in? Analogy does not consist in an imperfect similarity of things to one another, as it is commonly taken. For in this case that would be something very uncertain. Not only would we have bad predicates, because we would not be in a position to think of the reality itself without any limitations, but we could only ascribe these not wholly purified realities to God insofar as he had something perfectly similar to them in himself. But how would that help me? Could it give me a sufficiently complete concept of God? If, however, we assume analogy to be the perfect similarity of relations (not of things, but of relations) or, in short, what the mathematicians understand as *proportion*, then we will be satisfied at once. We can then form a concept of God and of his predicates which will be so sufficient that we will never need anything more. But obviously we will not assume any relations of magnitude (for this belongs to mathematics). Rather, we will assume a relation of cause and effect, or even better, of ground and consequence, so that we are able to argue in a wholly philosophical manner.[5] For just as in the world one thing is regarded as the cause of another thing when it contains the ground for this thing, so in the same way, we regard the whole world as a consequence of its ground *in God*, and argue from the analogy. For instance, just as the happiness of one man (the canceling of his misery) is related to the benevolence of another, so in just the same way the happiness of all men is related to the benevolence of God.

[The Possibility of an *entis realissimi*]

The first ground of proof for the existence of God is the ontological one, from pure concepts. But the real possibility of a most

5. Kant's preference for the ground/consequence relation over the cause/effect relation is probably a critical reflection on Eberhard's discussion of the "way of causality" (*via causalitatis*) (Eberhard, *Vorbereitung*, p. 26). Kant rejects

perfect being must be proven before I can prove its existence in this way.[6] For the dogmatic atheist absolutely denies the possibility of a God, and asserts that there is no God. But here, where we have to do only with pure reason, denying the existence of an *entis realissimi* and denying its possibility are fundamentally the same thing. Hence if the dogmatic atheist denies that there is a God, he takes upon himself the obligation to prove that God is impossible. For all our a priori knowledge is of such a kind that when I presume to prove from pure reason that something does not exist, I can only do it by proving that it is impossible for this thing to exist. The reason for this is that since here I can borrow no proof from experience either for or against the existence of a being, it follows that I have no other path before me but to prove from the mere concept of the thing that it does not exist, and that means proving that the thing contradicts itself. Hence before he presumes the right to assert that no *ens realissimum* exists, the dogmatic atheist must show that an object corresponding to our idea of such a being would contradict itself in the unification of its predicates. On the other hand, if it occurs to us to want to demonstrate a priori that God does exist, then we too must undertake the duty to prove through pure reason and with apodictic certainty that God is possible. But there is no way we can do this except by proving that an *ens realissimum* does not contradict itself in the synthesis of all its predicates. But in his proof for the possibility of an *entis realissimi* Leibniz confused the possibility of this concept with the possibility of the thing itself. He argued as follows: In my concept of an *ente realissimo* there is no contradiction, because one reality cannot con-

---

it as employing an empirical concept (causality) where a pure concept of the understanding (ground and consequence) would be appropriate.

6. Duns Scotus was the first to maintain that the ontological argument depends on the assumption that the concept of God involves no contradiction. And Scotus rejected the argument because he held this assumption to be unprovable. (Duns Scotus, *Commentaria Oxoniensis*. Quarracchi, 1912–14, 1, 2, 2, no. 32). Leibniz accepted the challenge, and offered a proof that the concept of God is necessarily free of contradiction (Leibniz, *Philosophischen Schriften*, ed. Gerhardt, vol. 7, pp. 261–262. Cf. Loemker, ed., Leibniz, *Philosophical Papers and Letters* [Dordrecht, 1969], p. 167). Kant accepts Leibniz's proof, but insists that it demonstrates only the logical possibility of a perfect being and not its real possibility.

tradict another. For a contradiction necessarily requires a negation in order for me to say that something both is and is not. But where there are only sheer realities, there is no negation and hence no contradiction either. But if there is no contradiction in the concept of an *ente realissimo*, then such a thing is possible. Leibniz should have concluded, however, only that my idea of such a thing is possible. For the fact that there is nothing contradictory in my concept of a thing does prove that it is the concept of something possible, but it does not yet prove the possibility of the object of my idea. The principle of contradiction is only the analytic principle of possibility, by means of which it is established with apodictic certainty whether my concept is possible or impossible. But it is not the synthetic principle of possibility, and by means of it we cannot prove at all whether or not the predicates of a thing would cancel each other in the thing itself. For I cannot come to know the synthesis of predicates in the object by means of the principle of contradiction. This knowledge would have to come rather from an insight into the constitution and range of each predicate as regards its operations. Hence if I undertake to prove the possibility of an *entis realissimi* (that is, to prove the possibility of the synthesis of all predicates in one object), then I presume to prove a priori through my reason and with apodictic certainty that all perfections can be united in a single stem and derived from a single principle. But such a proof transcends the possible insight of all human reason. For where will I get this knowledge? From the world? All right, but in the world I will find realities only as they are dispersed among objects. For example, one person has a great capacity for understanding, but is somewhat indecisive; another has very lively affections but only an average amount of insight. In animals I note an astonishing fertility in propagation, but no reason; in man I find reason but much less fertility. In short, I see in these cases that where one reality is found, some other reality is not present. Now obviously I cannot infer from them that the one reality cancels the other, and conclude for instance that it is impossible for there to be a man who unites in himself every reality a man can have. But on the other hand, I also have no insight as to how such a perfect human being could be possible. For I cannot know whether in the synthesis (the composition) of all human realities the effects of one perfection would contradict the effects of another. In order to have this insight I would have to know all the possible effects of these single realities. But I do not perceive all their possible effects in a synthesis of all human realities. Applying this to God, I must all the more admit my inability to see how a synthesis of all possible realities could be possible as regards their effects. For how can my reason presume to know how all the highest realities operate, what effects would arise from them, and what sort of relation all these realities would have to each other? But I would have to be able to know this if I wanted to see whether or not all realities could be united together in one object. And only this would show me whether God is possible.

On the other hand, however, it is also impossible for human reason ever to prove that such a combination of all perfections in one thing is *not* possible. For this would also require an insight into the range of the effects of the total reality. Hence the same grounds which put before our eyes the inability of human reason to assert the existence of such a being are also necessary and sufficient to prove that no counterassertion of God's nonexistence can be made either.

In short, it is impossible to prove that God is impossible. On the contrary, reason does not put the least obstacle in the way of my assuming the possibility of a God, if I should feel bound to do so in some other way. Reason itself is not able to prove with apodictic certainty that God is possible (and a priori proofs must one and all have apodictic certainty, otherwise they are not proofs). For this would require an insight which far transcends the bounds of the human faculty of reason. But from this same inability of my reason follows the impossibility ever of proving that a most perfect being is not possible. Hence the edifice of the dogmatic atheist falls to the ground. For if he wishes to deny God's existence and assert that there absolutely is no God, the atheist must first demonstrate the impossibility of God. But here reason forsakes him, and everything he may bring against the possibility of God will be only so much absurdity and nonsense. From all this we see that human reason can prove neither the possibility nor the impossibility of God, because it lacks the necessary insight into the range and effects of all realities. But nothing prevents us from assuming the possibility of God, if we should be able to find convincing grounds for it in some other way.

Now just as we can refute the dogmatic atheist and reject his presumptuous assertions of the nonexistence of God before we ourselves have proven that God exists, so in the same way we can also render fruitless all the assaults of the skeptical atheist without previously giving a proof for the existence of a most perfect being. For since he knows that speculative reason cannot prove the existence of God to our satisfaction, the skeptical atheist doubts that any sort of proof for it can be found, and so he also doubts God's existence itself. The skeptical atheist can be refuted only if, granting him the insufficiency of all speculative proofs for the existence of God as an *entis realissimi*, we nonetheless feel an inner conviction on *practical* grounds that a God *must* exist. We must assume there is a God and we must believe in him, even though our reason may not venture to assume his possibility and his existence a priori.

[The A Priori Proofs]

The ontological proof for the existence of a God is taken from the concept of an *entis realissimi*. The argument is this: An *ens realissimum* is something which contains all realities in itself. But existence is also a reality. Hence the *ens realissimum* must necessarily exist. Thus if someone were to assert that God does not exist, he would be negating in the predicate something which is included in the subject, and this would be a contradiction. The great simplicity of this proof by itself provokes suspicion; and the suspicion is not unfounded. But we will let the critique of the proof take its course, and see whether the proof holds water.

In this proof, everything unquestionably depends on whether the existence of a thing is in fact one of its realities. But the fact that a thing exists does not by itself make the thing more perfect. By existing, the thing does not contain any new predicate. Rather it is only posited with all its predicates. The thing was already just as complete in my concept when I thought of it as possible, as it is afterward when it actually exists. For otherwise, if existence were a special reality belonging to the thing, it would not be the same thing I had thought before, but more would exist in it than was included in the concept of the object. *Being* is thus obviously not a real predicate, that is, the concept of something which could be added to the concept of a thing in order to make it still more perfect. It is only the positing of a thing, or of certain determinations, in themselves. In its logical employment, it is merely the copula of a judgment. The proposition *God is omnipotent* contains only two concepts which have objects, God and omnipotence. The little word *is* is not a further predicate, but is only that which posits the predicate (omnipotent) in relation to the subject (God). If I now take the subject (God) together with all its predicates (including omnipotence) and say *God exists* or *There is a God*, I do not add any new predicate to the concept of God. Rather I only posit the subject in itself with all its predicates, and the object in relation to my concept. Both the object and the concept must have the same content, and thus nothing can be added to the concept (which expresses mere possibility) by simply thinking its object as given (through the expression *it is*). Hence the actual contains no more than the merely possible. For example, one hundred actual dollars do not contain the least bit more than one hundred possible dollars. For the possible dollars signify the concept, and the actual ones, the object of this concept and the positing of it as such. Hence in a case where the object contained more than the concept, my concept would not express the whole object, and thus would not be the concept appropriate to it. The object in its actuality is not contained analytically in my concept, but is added synthetically to my concept (which is a determination of my state). But this additional *being* external to my concept does not in the least increase the hundred dollars I am thinking of. Whatever our concept of an object may contain and however much it may contain, we must still go beyond it if we are to impart existence to the object. If I think in a thing every reality except one, the missing reality is not added if I say that this defective thing exists. On the contrary, it exists with precisely the same deficiency I have thought in it, for otherwise what exists would be something different from what I was thinking of. Now if I think of some being as the highest reality (without deficiency), it is still an open question whether it exists or not.[7] For it is just as thoroughly determined as an ideal as it would be if it were an actual object. From this we see how rash it would be to conclude that existence is comprehended in all reality, and hence that existence is included already in the concept of a possible thing. And thus collapses every argument which says that existence follows necessarily from the concept of an *entis realissimi*.

The cosmological proof retains the connection of absolute necessity and the highest reality. But instead of inferring necessary existence from supreme reality, it infers from an already given unconditional necessity of some being to its unbounded reality. Leibniz, and later Wolff, called this the proof *a contingentia mundi* [from the contingency of the world]. It says that if something exists, then an absolutely necessary being must also exist. But at the very least, I myself exist. Therefore, an absolutely necessary being exists. The minor premise of this argument contains an experience, and the major premise contains an inference from experience. This inference rests on the natural law of causality, which says that everything contingent has a cause. This cause, if it is also contingent, must once again have a cause, and so on. This series of things subordinated one to another has to end in an absolutely necessary cause, since otherwise it would not be complete. For a *regressus in infinitum*, a series of effects without a supreme cause, is absurd. Everything which exists can only exist in one of two ways, either *contingently* or *necessarily*. Whatever is contingent must have some cause for its existing as it does and not otherwise. But I myself (and even the world in general) exist contingently. Hence an absolutely necessary being must also exist, in order to be the cause of my being as I am and not otherwise. Thus the proof really does begin from an experience, and so it is not carried out in a wholly a priori manner, or ontologically. And it is called the *cosmological* proof because the object of any possible experience is called a

7. Cf. *Critique of Pure Reason*, A598-600/B626-628.

world. But since it abstracts from every particular attribute which distinguishes this world from any other possible world and founds itself only on a world in general without regard to its constitution, the cosmological proof is distinguished in its denomination from the physicotheological proof, which makes use of observations about the particular constitution of the sensible world as grounds of proof. But the cosmological proof argues further from the existence of an absolutely necessary being to the conclusion that this being must also be an *ens realissimum*. This argument runs as follows. A necessary being can only be determined in one way: that is, with respect to all possible *praedicatorum contradictorie oppositorum* [contradictorily opposed predicates] it must be determined by one of these opposed predicates. Consequently, it must be thoroughly determined by its concept. But there is only one possible concept of a thing which determines it thoroughly a priori, and this is the concept of the *entis realissimi*. For in every possible pair of *praedicatis contradictorie oppositis*, only the reality always belongs to it. Hence the concept of a most real being is the only concept by means of which a necessary being can be thought. Or in other words, there exists an *ens realissimum* and it exists necessarily.[8]

The cosmological proof bases itself on experience and gives itself the appearance of arriving step by step at the existence of a necessary being in general. But the empirical concept can teach us nothing about the attributes of this being. On the contrary, at this point reason says goodbye to experience and searches only among concepts. For if I ask what attributes a necessary being must have, the answer can only be: those attributes from which its absolute necessity flows. But reason believes that the requisites needed for absolute necessity are met with solely in the concept of a most real being. So it concludes that the absolutely necessary being is the most real being. But how could reason conclude this if it had not already *presupposed* that the concept of a being of the highest reality is fully adequate to the concept of absolute necessity? This proposition, which was asserted in the ontological argument, is thus assumed in the cos-

8. Ibid., A605f/B633f.

mological and made the ground for its proof, even though it was supposed to be denied.

But since the absolutely necessary existence of a highest reality could not be successfully proven from the concept to which this object corresponds, it will also be impossible conversely to demonstrate successfully the supreme reality of a thing from its absolute necessity. For absolute necessity is an existence from mere concepts. If I say that the concept of an *entis realissimi* is a concept of this kind and in fact the only concept fitting and adequate to necessary existence, then I must also admit that existence can be inferred from the concept of a most real being. Thus really only the ontological proof from mere concepts is contained in the so-called cosmological power of proof, and the supposed experience is wholly superfluous. It serves, perhaps, to lead us to the concept of absolute necessity, but not to establish this concept as pertaining to any determinate thing. For as soon as this is our intention, we must immediately leave all experience behind and seek among pure concepts for those which contain the possibility of an absolutely necessary being. If it were correct that every absolutely necessary being is also a most real being, then it would also be possible to convert the proposition, as can be done with every affirmative judgment, and to say that every most real being is a necessary being. Now since this proposition is determined a priori from mere concepts, the mere concept of an *entis realissimi* must carry its own absolute necessity along with it. This is asserted by the ontological proof, but the cosmological proof does not want to recognize it, even though it secretly underlies the inferences made in this proof.

[Necessary Existence]

But what sort of concept do we have of an absolutely necessary being or thing? In all ages men have spoken of an absolutely necessary being, but they have not taken the trouble to understand whether and how they could think of such a thing at all. Instead, they have straightway tried to prove its existence. An explanation of the name of this concept is quite easy to give; it is something whose nonexistence is impossible. But this explanation makes us none the wiser as to the conditions which might make it impossible for this thing not to be.[9] For the human understanding cannot grasp how the nonexistence of a thing might be impossible,[10] since it has a concept of impossibility only through the principle of contradiction. For every contradiction, two parts are required; a single thing cannot contradict itself. Hence there can never be a contradiction in the nonexistence of a thing, consequently there is no contradiction in the nonexistence of an *entis realissimi*. In his explanation of the absolute necessity of the *entis realissimi*, Wolff[11] used as an example the fact that it is absolutely necessary that a triangle should have three angles. But the absolute necessity of this judgment is only a conditioned necessity of the matter or predicate in the judgment. The proposition in question does not say that three angles necessarily exist, but rather that under the condition that a triangle exists (is given), three angles necessarily exist along with it. If in an ideal judgment I cancel the predicate and retain the subject, a contradiction results. For instance, to posit a triangle and cancel its three angles is contradictory. Thus I say that this predicate belongs necessarily to the subject. But if I cancel the subject together with the predicate, no contradiction results. For nothing is left which could be contradicted. Thus, for example, there is no contradiction in canceling the triangle together with its three angles. And this has direct application to the concept of an absolutely necessary being. If I cancel its existence, I cancel the thing itself with all its predicates. So where can the contradiction come from? There is nothing external to it which could be contradicted, for the thing is not supposed to be externally necessary. But there is also no internal contradiction, for by canceling the thing itself I have at the same time canceled everything internal to it.

9. Ibid., A592-596/B621-624.

10. Pölitz's text reads *möglich*. I presume this is an error, and Kant means *unmöglich*.

11. I am unable to locate any passage in Wolff where this illustration is employed, but of course it is employed by Descartes in connection with his proof for God's existence in *Meditations* V. It seems reasonable to suppose, therefore, that it is Descartes and not Wolff who is meant here, though it is impossible to say whether the error should be attributed to Pölitz, to Kant's transcriber, or to Kant himself.

For instance: *God is omnipotent*. This is a necessary judgment. Omnipotence cannot be canceled as long as I posit a Deity with whose concept this predicate is identical. Here I have logically unconditioned necessity. But now what would an absolute real necessity have to be? It would have to consist in its being absolutely necessary that God must exist. But if I say that God does not exist, then neither omnipotence nor any other of his predicates is given. For they are all canceled along with the object, and this thought does not exhibit the least contradiction. An internal contradiction can never arise from my canceling the predicate of a judgment along with the object, no matter what the predicate may be. Thus I cannot form the least concept of a thing which would leave a contradiction behind if it were canceled along with all its predicates. But apart from contradictions I have no mark of impossibility merely through pure concepts a priori. Hence in this case it is possible that God does not exist. It costs speculative reason nothing at all to cancel God's existence in thought. The whole task of the transcendental ideal depends on either finding a concept for absolute necessity or on finding absolute necessity in the concept of some thing. If we can do the one, we must be able to do the other as well. For reason knows absolute necessity only in what is necessary from its concept. But both tasks wholly transcend every effort of our understanding to satisfy itself over this point; yet at the same time they transcend every attempt to rest content with our incapacity. This absolute necessity which we need indispensably as a final ground for all things is the true abyss for human reason.[12] Even eternity, as described in its dreadful sublimity by a Haller, does not make so dizzying an impression on the mind.[13] For eternity

12. Ground = *Grund*. Abyss = *Abgrund*.

13. Victor Albrecht von Haller (1708–1777), Swiss anatomist and physiologist, was also a poet and novelist of some fame. The allusion is to Haller's *Unvollkommenes Gedicht über Ewigkeit* (Unfinished Poem on Eternity) (1736). In his 1794 essay "The End of All Things," Kant quotes the following lines from the poem: "*Ihn aber hält am ernsten Orte, / Der nichts zurücke lässt, / Die Ewigkeit mit starken Armen fest*." ("But in that earnest place, / Him who leaves nothing behind, / Eternity holds fast in its strong arms.") *Gesammelte Schriften*, vol. 8, p 327. (Cf. *Kant on History*, L. W. Beck, ed. [Indianapolis, 1963], p. 69.) Cf. *Critique of Pure Reason*, A613/B641, and *Gesammelte Schriften*, vol. 2, p. 151.

only *lacks* the duration of things; it does not *support* this duration. We can neither resist nor tolerate the thought of a being which we represent as the highest of all possible things, and which may say to itself, "I am from eternity to eternity, and outside me there is nothing except what exists through my will. But whence am I?" This thought pulls the ground from beneath us, and the greatest perfection as much as the smallest hovers without support before speculative reason. But it costs reason nothing to let both of them disappear, nor is there the least obstacle to this. In short, an absolutely necessary thing will remain to all eternity an insoluble problem for human reason.

Up to this point we have followed Eberhard's *Vorbereitung zur natürlichen Theologie [Propaedeutic to Natural Theology]*. But now he proceeds immediately to the physicotheological proof, and it seems to us more systematic not to pursue this subject quite yet. Instead, now that we have treated the concept of a highest being and the proof for the existence of this being from pure reason, we will proceed to the *ontological predicates* of this being, and we will treat of them in their connection with transcendental theology. The first consideration here is the *possibility* of God, which no one can either deny or prove, because such knowledge transcends all human reason. As was shown above, the objective reality of the synthesis which generates this concept rests on principles of possible experience. (And by *experience* we understand the sum total of all the objects of sense.) But how am I going to have a priori insight into the possibility of this thing without being able to perceive the synthesis of its predicates? As long as my concept does not contradict itself, it is possible. But this analytic principle (the principle of contradiction) is only the *logical* characteristic of possibility, by means of which an object can be distinguished from a *nihil negativo* [negative nothing]. But how can I straightway infer the possibility of a thing (real possibility) from the possibility of a concept (logical possibility)?

Let us now go on to the proof that the *ens realissimum* must also be the *ens entium*; or, as we expressed it earlier, that the most perfect being must contain in itself the ground of the possibility of all other things. We have already established this through the fact that everything which is a *partim reale, partim negativum* presupposes a being containing all realities in itself and constituting these things through a limitation of its realities. For otherwise we could not think where either the realities or the negations in things come from, because even a negation always presupposes some reality and arises through the limitation of this reality. On this point rests the only possible ground of proof for my demonstration of God's existence, which was discussed in detail in an essay I published some years ago.[14] Here it was shown that of all possible proofs, the one which affords us the most satisfaction is the argument that if we cancel an original being, we cancel at the same time the substratum of the possibility of all things. But even this proof is not apodictically certain. For it is unable to establish the objective necessity of an original being; rather it establishes only the subjective necessity of assuming such a being. But this proof can in no way be refuted, because it has its ground in the nature of human reason. For my reason makes it absolutely necessary for me to assume a being which is the ground of everything possible, because otherwise I would be unable to know what in general the possibility of something consists in.

Now since the highest being is also the original being from which the essence of all things is derived, it follows that the order, beauty, harmony, and unity which are met with in things are not always contingent, but inhere necessarily in their essence. For instance, we find that our earth is flattened at the poles but elevated between the tropics and the equator.[15] And this follows from the necessity of its nature, that is, from the equilibrium of the fluid masses of which the earth was once composed. Hence Newton could prove the shape of the earth reliably a priori and prior to experience, before the astronomers had measured its elevation at the equator merely given the fact that it once was in a fluid state. Moreover, this oblateness of the

14. *Der einzig mögliche Beweisgrund zu einer Demonstration des Daseins Gottes* (The Only Possible Ground of Proof for a Demonstration of God's Existence) (1763), *Gesammelte Schriften*, vol. 2, pp. 63–204.

15. Cf. *Critique of Pure Reason*, A637/6715.

spherical earth is of great advantage, since only it prevents the projections of solid earth (or even smaller mountains perhaps raised by earthquakes) from continuously displacing the earth's axis, perhaps even to a noticeable degree over a long period of time. For the rotation of the earth at the equator is, so to speak, such a mighty mountain that the vibration of all the other mountains will never noticeably alter the earth's position in relation to its axis, or even be able to alter it. But wise as this arrangement is, I may not account for it as a contingent act of the divine will. For, as we have just actually established, it must be regarded as necessary to the nature of the earth. Yet this takes nothing away from God's majesty as creator of the world. For since he is the original being from whose essence the nature of all things is derived, the necessity of this natural arrangement is also derived from his essence. But it is not derived from his will, since in that case he would only be the world's architect, and not its creator. Only what is contingent in things can be derived from the divine will and its arbitrary directives. But everything contingent is contained in the form of things; consequently, only the form of things can be derived from the divine will. To say this is not to make things themselves independent of God, nor is it to withdraw them in any way from his highest supreme power. For by regarding God as the *ens originarium* containing in itself the ground of all possible things, we derive the matter of things from the divine essence, since this matter consists in realities. Thus we make the essence of things themselves derivative from God, that is, from his essence. For it is unthinkable that a special divine volition could be necessary to produce certain effects in a thing which follow necessarily from its nature. For instance, how could a special divine volition be necessary to give a spheroid shape to a fluid body revolving on its axis? For this is a necessary effect of the body's own nature. If we wanted to derive everything from the divine will, we would have to make everything inhering necessarily in the nature of things independent of God. We would have to recognize a creator only for what is contingent, that is, only for the *form* of things, and not for their matter or for what belongs necessarily to the things themselves. Hence if the laws and arrangements in nature which flow from the essence of things themselves are to be dependent on God (and they must be dependent on him, since otherwise we would be unable to find any ground for their possibility), then they can only be derived from his original essence.

From everything which has been brought forth thus far from pure reason in favor of God's existence, we see that we are justified in assuming and presupposing an *ens originarium* which is at the same time an *ens realissimum* as a necessary transcendental hypothesis. For to cancel a being which contains the data for everything possible is to cancel all possibility. And therefore a most real original being is a necessary presupposition, on account of its relationship to the possibility of all things. For in addition to the logical concept of the necessity of a thing (where something is said to be absolutely necessary if its nonexistence would be a contradiction, and consequently impossible), we have yet another rational concept of real necessity. This is where a thing is *eo ipso* necessary if its nonexistence would cancel all possibility. Of course in the logical sense possibility always precedes actuality, and here I can think the possibility of a thing without actuality. Only we have no concept of real possibility except through existence, and in the case of every possibility which we think *realiter* we always presuppose some existence; if not the actuality of the thing itself, then at least an actuality in general containing the data for everything possible. Hence every possibility presupposes something actually given. For if everything were merely possible, then the possible itself would have no ground. Consequently this ground of possibility must itself be given not merely as possible, but also as actual.

But it must be noted that this proof only establishes the subjective necessity of such a being. That is, our speculative reason sees that it is necessary to presuppose this being if it wants to have insight into *why* something is possible. But the objective necessity of such a thing can by no means be demonstrated in this manner. For here reason must come to know its weakness, its inability to soar above the bounds of all possible experience. And insofar as it does presume to continue its flight beyond these bounds, it only falls into whirlpools and turbulent waters, plunging it into a bottomless abyss where it is wholly swallowed up.

Hence the totality of what speculative reason can teach us concerning the existence of God consists in showing us how we must necessarily hypothesize this existence. But speculative reason does not show us how God's existence could be demonstrated with apodictic certainty. Even this much is quite fortunate for us, since it removes every obstacle which might stand in the way of our assuming a being of all beings. Indeed, if we can be convinced of such a being in some other way, we can believe in it firmly and unshakeably. For even in the speculative use of reason, the highest being remains an ideal free from faults, anchoring and crowning the whole of human knowledge.

[God's Ontological Attributes]

According to Baumgarten, all the attributes of God are either *quiescentes* [at rest] or *operativae* [active].[16] *Perfectiones quiescentes* are those in which we think of an action which can be represented without a *nota actionis* [mark of activity]. *Operatives*, on the other hand, cannot be thought without some characteristic of an activity. Let us first consider God's *perfectiones quiescentes*, since his ontological predicates belong to them. In addition to God's possibility and actuality, which we have already treated as far as reason can teach us about them, we further maintain that God is a *substance*. This predicate belongs to God merely as a thing, since all things are substances. A substance is understood to be a reality existing merely for itself, without being a determination of any other thing. A substance is opposed to an accident, which can only exist by inhering in another thing. *Accidentia* are therefore not particular things, but only different ways or *modi* of the existence of a substance. But God is a thing for itself and *eo ipso* a substance. If we wanted to dispute God's substantiality, we would have to deny him thinghood as well,

16. Some of God's attributes, such as substantiality, simplicity, and immutability, can be represented without a *nota actionis* (a mark of activity), while others, such as omnipotence, freedom, and wisdom, cannot. The former perfections Baumgarten calls *perfectiones quiescentes*, and the latter *perfectiones operativae* (*Metaphysica*, §815).

and thus cancel the whole concept of God. But if God is assumed to be an *ens realissimum*, then it follows already just from the concept of a thing that God is a substance.

Another of God's ontological predicates is *unity*.[17] For as the most real being, God is thoroughly determined in that in each pair of *praedicatis contradictorie oppositis* only the reality belongs to him. Now this concept of a being having every reality can only be *singularis*. It can never be thought as a species, for in every species the individuals must somehow be distinguished from each other if they are to be particular things. But this distinction can only take place through a distribution of reality. In other words, one thing must have something in itself which the others do not. But this contradicts our concept of the *realissimo*.

From God's unity follows his *simplicity*.[18] For every *compositum reale* [composite of real things] is to be regarded as reality composed of substances external to each other and yet standing *in commercio* [in reciprocal interaction]. Hence if God is to be *compositum*, he must consist of many parts. Now either each of these parts would be an *ens realissimum* (and then there would be many *realissima*, which is a contradiction); or else the parts would be *partim realia, partim negativa*. But in this case the whole consisting of these parts would also be only a *partim reale, partim negativum*, and consequently not a *realissimum* and not God. For an unlimited reality can never arise out of many limited realities, because in order for a thing to have unlimited reality, all realities must be united in one subject. It is just this unification, therefore, which constitutes the form of an *entis realissimi*. But as soon as realities are distributed (and there must be such a distribution among the parts of the *compositi* if the *enis realissimum* is to be an *ens compositum*), then limitations arise. For whenever a reality is distributed among several things, the whole reality cannot be in each of them, and consequently each part lacks some of the reality. The unity of a *compositi* is always only a contingent unity

17. "To God belongs the highest unity, which is inseparable from the plurality of the highest realities" (Baumgarten, *Metaphysica*, §815).

18. "Every substance is a monad. God is a substance. Hence God is a monad and a simple being. But if the highest simplicity of God is granted, then it is denied that there could be any ground for his being a composite, made up of external parts" (Baumgarten, *Metaphysica*, §838).

of combination. Hence the parts of every composite can always be represented separately. If in fact they are combined, it still could have been otherwise. But the unity of a simple substance is necessary. Thus the simplicity of the *entis realissimi* can also be proven from its absolute necessity. For if the *ens realissimum* were an *ens compositum*, then all its parts would have to be absolultely necessary if the whole is to be absolutely necessary. For the whole cannot be constituted in a manner different from the parts of which it consists. But then there would be many *entia absolute necessaria*, which contradicts the concept of absolute necessity. A third proof for the simplicity of God is derived from the fact that every *compositum* is also *divisibile*, in that it consists of parts. But divisibility always involves the inner changeableness of a thing, since the relation between the parts of an *ente composito* can be changed. Hence every composite substance is internally changeable. But this contradicts the concept of an *ente realissimo*. Now it follows also that because the most real being must be simple, it must be immaterial as well. For matter is what constitutes anything composite.

Further, *immutability* belongs to God, and is one of his *perfectionibus quiescentibus*. But immutability as a concept should not be confused with the immutable as a thing. Baumgarten has not duly observed this distinction. For he infers the unchangeableness of God from the fact that every determination of a most real being is absolutely and internally unchangeable.[19] But from this fact it follows only that the concept of God is transcendentally unchangeable in that God is thoroughly determined through his concept.

But what is change or mutation? It is a succession of states. So changes can only be thought possible in time, for only here is there succession. If we want to prove the unchangeableness of God, then we first have to prove that God is not in time. But this can be seen clearly from the concept of an *entis realissimi*. For if God were in time he would have to be limited. But he is a *realissimus*, and consequently he is not in time. God's real unchange-

19. "The determinations of every necessary being are absolutely and internally immutable. Therefore, God is absolutely and internally immutable" (Baumgarten, *Metaphysica*, §839).

ableness also follows from his absolute necessity. For if God were so constituted that something could arise in him which was not already actual, then it could not be said that he is necessary in his actual constitution. For he could have been otherwise than he is, since he could be sometimes in one state and sometimes in another. From this highest immutability of God with respect to all his realities it follows that it is anthropomorphic to represent God as being first wrathful and then merciful. For this would be to suppose a change in God. But God is and remains always the same, equally merciful and equally just. It depends on us alone whether we are to become objects of his mercy or of his punitive justice. The change takes place within *us*. It is our relation to God which is changed. If we better ourselves and alter our previous relation to God as culpable sinners to a just God, then after our improvement this relation will be canceled and will be replaced by a relation of upright friends of virtue. It does not accord with the concept of an unchangeable God that God should be more effective in us just because we make moral betterment our end. Rather, when we work for our betterment, it is we ourselves who are more susceptible to the influence of his power, and we participate in it to a higher degree. His influence itself does not increase or become stronger, because this would be a change in him. But we feel it to be stronger, because we no longer resist it. Yet the influence itself remains the same.

Baumgarten next discusses polytheism.[20] It doubtless arose because men could not comprehend the apparent conflict of purposes in the world, the mixture of good and evil. So they assumed several beings as the cause of this conflict and assigned to each a special department. Nevertheless, in addition to these lower gods every heathen people has the thought of a special original source out of which they flowed. But they made this supreme principle in and for itself so blessed that it has nothing at all to do with the world. Examples of this are the Tibetans and other existing heathen people of inner Asia. And in fact they follow the course of human reason, which needs a thoroughgoing

20. "Many gods are impossible . . . God is unique. POLYTHEISM is the proposition positing more than one god, and is an error" (Baumgarten, *Metaphysica*, §846).

unity in its representation and cannot stop until it has reached the One which is higher than everything. Polytheism as such, not combined with a supreme original source, would be in conflict with common human understanding. For common sense teaches monotheism by taking as its supreme principle a being which is all in all. Thus it should not be thought that the doctrine of one God needs to be built on a very advanced human insight. It is rather a need of the most common reason. Hence it was something universally acknowledged even in the beginning. But since men subsequently perceived many kinds of destructive forces in the world, they did not believe that these forces along with the agreement and harmony in nature could be derived from one God. So they assumed various lower gods and ascribed special operations to each one. And since everything in the world carries with it something which can be put under the rubric of either good or evil, they assumed a divine duality, a *principium bonum et malum*. And this was *manichaeism*.[21] But this doctrine does not seem so wholly nonsensical and absurd if we consider that the manichaeans also posited a supreme principle beyond this duality, from which it had arisen. It would have been absurd, however, if they had made the two principles into a *realissimis*, since it would be contradictory for an *ens realissimum* to be a *principium malum*. Yet they did not think of either principle as a *realissimum*, but gave some realities to one and other realities to the other. Consequently negations could be thought in both their principles. But above these *principiis partim realibus, partim negativis* they thought of a supreme original source of everything, an *ens realissimum*. From this we can see that polytheism did not cancel monotheism, but both could be combined without contradiction, since different concepts were bound up with the term *God*.

Now let us proceed to another ontological predicate of the *entis realissimi*, which is also one of its *perfectiones quiescentes*. This perfection consists in its being *extramundanum*.[22] To this perfection belong the following two points:

21. "MANICHAEISM is the proposition positing an equally powerful god as the author of evil, and is an error" (Baumgarten, *Metaphysica*, §844).

22. "God is a being outside the world (*ens extramundanum*). And the world

(1) God is an *ens a mundo diversum*, or external to the world in an intellectual way. This proposition is opposed to Spinozism, for Spinoza believed that God and the world were one substance and that apart from the world there is no substance at all. This error flowed from his faulty definition of substance. As a mathematician, he was accustomed to finding arbitrary definitions and deriving propositions from them. Now this procedure does work quite well in mathematics, but if we try to apply these methods to philosophy we will be led into error.[23] For in philosophy we must first seek out the characteristics themselves and acquaint ourselves with them before we can construct their definitions. But Spinoza did not do this. Instead, he constructed an arbitrary definition of substance. *Substantia*, he said, *est cujus existentia non indiget existentia alterius*.[24] Assuming this definition, he correctly inferred that there is only one substance, God. But everything in the world is an *accidens* inhering in this divinity, since each thing has need of God's existence for its own existence. Consequently everything existing is in God and nothing can be or be thought as external to God. But this only means that God and the world are one. For the whole world is in God and nothing is outside him. Now this argument is just as mistaken in its content as it is correct in its form. For it is derived from a wholly false principle, from a faulty definition of substance. But we have already given another account of substance, and its correctness is clear because it is not assumed arbitrarily (like Spinoza's) but is derived instead from the concept of a thing itself. The concept of a thing in general teaches us that

is not something essential to him, nor is it his essence, nor one of God's attributes, nor modes, nor modifications, nor accidents. THEOLOGICAL SPINOZISM is the proposition denying that God is a being outside the world, and is an error" (Baumgarten, *Metaphysica*, §855).

23. Cf. *Critique of Pure Reason*, A727f/B755f.

24. "Substance is that whose existence does not require the existence of anything else." Kant is not quoting Spinoza accurately. *Ethics*, Part I, definition III, actually reads: *Per substantiam intelligo id, quod in se est et per se concipitur: hoc est id, cujus conceptus non indiget conceptu alterius rei, a quo formari debet*. That is: "By substance, I understand that which is in itself and is conceived through itself; it is that whose concept can be formed without requiring the concept of any other thing" (Spinoza, *Opera* [The Hague, 1882], I, p. 39).

everything real which exists for itself without being a determination of any other things, is a substance. Consequently all things are substances. For my own self-consciousness testifies that I do not[25] refer all my actions to God as the final subject which is not the predicate of any other thing. Hence the concept of a substance arises when I perceive in myself that I am not the predicate of any other thing. For instance: when I think, I am conscious that my ego thinks in me, and not in some other thing. So I conclude that my thinking does not inhere in another thing external to me, but inheres in myself. Consequently I conclude that I am a substance, that is, that I exist for myself and am not the predicate of any other thing. I myself am a thing, and thus also a substance. But now if I myself am a substance, then either I must be God himself or God is a substance different from me, and consequently different from the world. The first supposition is absurd, because it contradicts the concept of an *entis realissimi*. Consequently there must exist apart from me some other thing existing for itself which is not a predicate of any other existing thing. That is, there must be another existing substance. Indeed, apart from me there may be many other different substances, because infinitely many things are possible besides myself. But each thing, just because it is a thing, is *eo ipso* not a predicate of any other thing. Instead, it exists for itself and is thus a substance. Now all these things are distinguished from each other, because otherwise they would not be particular things. Hence an *ens realissimum* (which is already considered as a thing in having the highest reality) must also exist for itself and not be a predicate of another thing. That is, it must be a substance distinguished from every other. Taken together, the things which are comprehended in the world are all substances, because they would have to cease being things if they were mere determinations of some other thing. Consequently the whole world will not be a determination of God. Rather, the *ens realissimum* must be distinguished from it.

25. Pölitz's text reads: *Denn das Bewusstsein meiner selbst zeugt, dass ich alle Handlungen auf Gott, als auf das letzte Subject . . . beziehe. . . .* (There appears to be a *nicht* left out of the sentence.)

(2) God is an *ens extramundanum*. That is, he does not belong to the world at all, but is wholly outside it. This doctrine is opposed to the stoic proposition that God is the *world-soul*. But if this were so, then God and the world would have to stand *in commercio*, that is, each would have to influence the other. So God would have to be not only active but also passive. But this sort of reciprocal operation would contradict God and his concepts as an *ente realissimo* and *necessario*. For an *ens absolute necessarium* is *independens*, and consequently also *impassibile* (not passive). But if the world is to have influence on God so as to affect him, then *eo ipso* he would have to be dependent on the world. Man, of course, can only intuit an object insofar as he has the receptivity enabling him to be affected by it. But such an intuition cannot be predicated of God, because a limitation is comprehended in it.

Thus God is isolated. Yet not in the sense that he stands in no connection with the world at all, but rather only in the sense that he stands in no connection involving a *reciprocal* causality (of a *commercii*). Thus God has an influence on the world, he is active. But the world has no influence on him, that is, he is not passive. We have already dealt with God's *infinity* in the metaphysical sense, and it was shown above that instead of this one could better say that God has *all-sufficiency*. For the latter is a concept of the pure understanding, while the former is borrowed from mathematics and even belongs only to it.

Now let us consider God's *eternity*.[26] The magnitude of existence is duration. Hence we can combine the concept of magnitude with existence only through the mediation of time. For this is the measure of duration. Now *eternity* is: duration without

26. "In God there are no successive states. Hence God is not in time. . . . If a contingently eternal being be posited, its eternity differs in many ways from God's eternity. For (1) its duration as a continuous modification of successive states is obnoxious [to the divine nature]. (2) Its eternity has no protensive end; yet such an eternity could not really be called infinite. And (3) its eternity would be time without beginning or end (and could be called infinite for this reason); yet it is not really infinite mathematically. For a being having successive states is never actually all that it can be in its internal determinations" (Baumgarten, *Metaphysica*, §§849–850).

beginning or end. But what *is* beginning? What *is* end? Beginning is an existence. Very well. But what does this mean if not that before the beginning of a thing there was a time when it was not, or that after its end there will be a time when it is no more? Here, therefore, I still have a concept of time, and we cannot find a concept of eternity which would not still be affected with the concept of time. For beginning and end are only possible in time. The divine existence, however, can never be thought of as determinable through time. For then we would have to represent God as a *phaenomenon*. But this would be an anthropomorphic predicate, unthinkable in an *ente realissimo* because it contains limitations in it. For the existence of a thing in time is always a succession of parts of time, one after the other. Duration in time is, so to speak, a continuous disappearing and a continuous beginning. We can never live through[27] a certain year without having already lived through a previous one. But none of this can be said of God, since he is unchangeable. Hence since it is a continuous limitation, time must be opposed in quality to an *ente realissimo*. But if I represent eternity as a duration without beginning or end (which is about the most minimal account of eternity I can give), the concept of time is still mixed in. For duration, beginning, and end are all predicates which can only be thought of things in time. Of course it is true that I am negating beginning and end in relation to God. But I do not gain much by this fact, since my concept of eternity is not in the least enlightened or purified through such negations. Fundamentally I am still representing God as a being within time, even if I do remove beginning and end from him. But it is most necessary to leave all the conditions of time out of the concept of God, because otherwise we could be misled and accept a number of anthropomorphic consequences. For instance, if I think of God as existing within time but having no beginning or end, it is impossible for me to think how God could have created the world without suffering any change. Or again, I might ask what God was doing before there was a world. But if I reject all

27. Live through = *erleben*.

the conditions of time, then this *before* and *after* are concepts which cannot be thought in God at all. Hence even if I must be content to have very little comprehension of God's eternity, my concept may still be pure and free from errors, even though it is incomplete.

Some have tried to prevent the difficulties which arise from representing God's existence as within time, by insisting that all the consecutiveness of time be thought as simultaneous in God. But this pretension challenges us to think a contradiction. *Consecutive* states of a thing, which are nevertheless *simultaneous*. What is this, if not a *contradictio in adjecto*? *Simultaneously* means: at one time. Hence to think of consecutive parts of time as occurring at one time is contradictory. From all this we can see that if eternity is to be represented as a special attribute of God, it is still impossible to think of it apart from time, because time itself is a condition of all our representations, a form of sensibility. If we nevertheless want to exclude time from the concept of God, then little remains of eternity except a representation of the necessity of his existence. But we have to make do with this on account of the weakness of our reason. For it would be impertinent for us to want to lift the curtain which veils in holy darkness him who is invariably and forever. We must eliminate every sensible representation of time from the concept of God, because such representations can easily corrupt a concept which is supposed to be free from all limitation. But if we do eliminate them, then to be *eternal* means only: to be *absolutely necessary*. Now although we have seen that we are unable even to think this absolute necessity conceptually, it is nevertheless a concept reason necessitates us to assume before it can find rest.

Eternity has a great similarity to *omnipresence*. Just as our sensible representation of eternity fills all of time, so according to our sensible representation God's presence fills all of space. Hence the spatial presence of God, or God's presence in space, is subject to just the same difficulties as is his eternity when it is conjoined with time. For it is a contradiction that a thing should be in more than one place in space at the same time.

God's *omnipotence* is usually understood as his capacity to make possible things actual.[28] But it would be most presumptuous to test the power of God on things which are in themselves contradictory (such as a circle with four corners) and conclude that God is not capable of them. It would be foolish and frivolous to think of a being with supreme dignity and majesty in relation to *non entia*. In general there is something very improper about human reason presuming to dispute stubbornly about God, the most sublime thing which it can think only feebly, and wanting to represent everything of him, even the impossible. For whenever reason wants to venture into thoughts of this magnitude, it ought first to make a modest retreat and, fully conscious of its own incapacity, to take counsel with itself as to how it might worthily think of God. Hence all such expressions are presumptuous, even if they are only posited as hypotheses; for instance, some dare to picture God as a tyrant who makes the punishments of hell eternal or (according to the doctrine of predestination) who unconditionally determines some men to blessedness and others to damnation.

[The Value of Transcendental Theology]

Anthropomorphism is usually divided into the *vulgar* sort (where God is thought of in human shape) and the *subtle* sort (where human perfections are ascribed to God, but without separating the limitations from them).[29] The latter sort of anthropomorphism is a particularly dangerous enemy of our pure knowledge of God, since vulgar anthropomorphism is too obviously an error for men to be fooled by it very often. So we have to turn all our power against *anthropomorphismum subtilem*, because it is easier for it to creep into our concept of God and corrupt it. For it is better not to be able to represent something at all than only to be able to think of it confused with errors.

28. "Omnipotence is the force sufficient to actualize everything" (Baumgarten, *Metaphysica*, §832).

29. "God has no shape (*figuram*). VULGAR ANTHROPOMORPHISM (*Anthropomorphismus crassior*) is the error of attributing some shape to God (e.g., the human). SUBTLE ANTHROPOMORPHISM (*Anthropomorphismus subtilor*) is the error of attributing to God the imperfections of finite things (e.g., of man)" (Baumgarten, *Metaphysica*, §848).

It is for this reason that the transcendental theology we have been treating is of such great utility. It puts us in a position to remove from our knowledge of God everything sensible inhering in our concepts. Or at least by its means we become conscious that if we predicate something of God which cannot be thought apart from the conditions of sensibility, then we must give a proper account of these predicates, even if we are not always in a position to represent them in a manner wholly free from faults. It would be easiest to deal successfully with all the consequences of anthropomorphism if only our reason voluntarily relinquished its claim to know the nature of God and his attributes according to their inner constitution, and if our reason, mindful of its weakness, never tried to exceed its bounds, but was content to know only so much as it has need for about him who must always remain the object of an eternal quest. This interest of humanity is best furthered and attained *per viam analogiam*, as we will see below.

With this we will conclude our discussion of ontotheology,[30] in which we have considered God as the *original being*. At times we have inferred this originality from the concept of the *entis realissimi*, and sometimes we have inferred conversely from the concept of the *entis originarii* to its highest reality. Our effort and caution in the knowledge of this speculative part of theology have been rewarded in that we may assume, at least as an undoubted *hypothesis* of speculative reason, that there is a God, an *ens realissimum* with all the predicates flowing from this concept. Moreover, we can be sure that no rational man could ever prove the contrary to us and tear down this our support of all human reason. And is this not better than boasting that we can know God and his properties apodictically through pure reason, while having to fear each attack of our opponents? For what reason has taught us about God is faultless and free from error. Without hesitation we may found our further investigation on this modest but correct knowledge, and we may build on it with trust. It is true that all we know of God in transcendental theology is the mere concept of a highest original ground. But

30. Pölitz's text reads *Ontologie*.

although this concept is useless for itself and without any additional knowledge, it is excellent when it is applied as the substratum of all theology.

Second Section: Cosmotheology

In our treatment of the ontological proof for God's existence, we have already taken the opportunity to deal with the cosmological proof. But we did this only in order to compare both proofs of transcendental theology, and to show the close kinship between them. Now let us try to set forth a more detailed account of the whole concept of God insofar as it can be derived from a foundation in experience, yet without determining more closely the world to which this experience belongs. Cosmotheology teaches us a theistic concept of God, since in it we come to know God as the supreme intelligence, as a highest being who is author of all things through understanding and freedom. The deist, in his concept of God, understands merely a blindly acting eternal nature as the root of all things, an original being, or a supreme cause of the world. But he does not venture to assert that God is the ground of all things through freedom. Since we are interested only in the concept of an author of the world, that is, in the concept of a living God, let us see whether reason can provide us with this theistic concept of God as a *summa intelligentia*. This knowledge will not be wholly pure and independent of experience, but the experience which has to be its foundation is the simplest experience there could be, the experience of our self. Hence now we will proceed to the psychological predicates borrowed from the nature of our own soul, and we will ascribe them to God after separating all the limits from them. But if in the case of ontological predicates derived a priori much caution was necessary to avoid mixing in external sensible representations, think how much care will be necessary now, when we are founding everything only on empirical principles, or at least when it is from objects of sense (such as we ourselves are) that we must abstract the determinations from which we are to form the concept of a highest intelligence. Now we will have to apply all our attention if the reality is not to escape from us along with the limitations, and if, instead of making our concept of God more perfect, we are not to make it impure by bringing negations into it. If we meet with any reality in ourselves which we are able to ascribe to a being which has all reality, then we must be very careful to avoid predicating of God the negative element inhering in that reality as it is found in us. This separation of everything limited from the real is often very difficult for us, and nothing of the whole reality may be left over. In this case, where nothing remains after the careful testing of the reality and the removal of every limit, it is self-evident that we cannot think of such a thing in God. But even if the reality which is brought out *via negationis* from some perfection in us is only very small, we still should not omit it from God as long as it contains a true reality. Instead, we must predicate it of God *per viam eminentiae*. In a case like this the way of analogy is especially appropriate. For it teaches us the perfect similarity between the relation of things in the world (where one is regarded as ground and the other as consequence) and the relation of God to the world which has its being from him.

[God's Knowledge]

Firstly, we find in our soul a faculty of knowledge. No one can doubt that it is a reality. Everyone holds it to be a great perfection in which he shares to some extent. Hence we must introduce it into our concept of an *entis realissimi* too, after all the limits inhering in it have been carefully separated out. From this it follows that no contradiction will arise from the addition of this reality to our concept of a most perfect being, since one reality does not cancel another in a concept. But if we unite a faculty of knowledge with other perfections in our concept of God, it still does not follow that this reality belongs to the thing itself, in the synthesis of all other predicates. For as was shown above, this would mean that we would have to be acquainted with every predicate of the thing and with all the effects of each, and we would have to know how all these predicates would relate to each other when they were actually put together. But such knowledge of a most perfect being is impossible for the human understanding. Thus we cannot prove with apodictic certainty that the reality of a faculty of knowledge does not cancel any of the other realities when put together with them.[31] But neither can any man ever prove the contrary, that in fact some reality in the thing itself would be canceled or limited in its effects if it were put in combination with a faculty of knowledge. For both transcend the faculty of human reason. In such cases, where it is equally impossible to prove either side apodictically, we are free to choose the alternative which has the most probability for us. And no one can deny that the concept of an *entis realissimi* itself gives us a much greater right to ascribe a faculty of knowledge to it than to exclude such a faculty from the total reality. Here we already have one undoubted reason on our side in the fact that nothing contradictory shows itself in our concept. And while it does not follow that the object itself is possible in reality, still we cannot see any reason why this reality should not belong to the synthesis of attributes of a most perfect being, even if we cannot prove it with apodictic certainty from our concept of an *ente realissimo*. The deist has nothing on his side when he denies it, because such a denial would require an insight into the nature of an *entis realissimi* which would transcend all human reason.

But we have in addition a stronger ground of proof that God has a faculty of knowledge, a ground derived from the *constitution* of an *entis realissimi*. And a ground of proof derived from that always has more strength than grounds of proof taken merely from the concept of an *entis realissimi*. We argue that an *ens originarium* containing within itself the ground of the possibility of all things must have a faculty of knowledge because it is the original source of beings which do have this faculty (for example, man). For how could something be derived from a being unless this original being itself had it? Thus the original being of all beings must have a faculty of knowledge. Of course

31. In the Danzig manuscript of the Lectures Kant attributes to Hume the conjecture that "perhaps the reality of understanding does not admit of being united with the other realities." (*Gesammelte Schriften*, vol. 28, 2, 2, p. 1266.) I am unable, however, to locate any passage in Hume where anything of the sort is said.

the deist might reply that there could be another kind of reality in the original source of things which might give rise to the faculty of knowledge inhering in human beings. In this case, the faculty of knowledge would not itself be an original reality, but would have to be only a consequence of some reality, unknown to us, in the original being. Thus the Tibetans, for instance, represent God as the highest source from which all other beings emanate and to which they will again return. But they do not ascribe to this original being the same perfections as belong to the things derived from it. But where will the deist find a reason for asserting such a thing? It is true that we can never refute him with apodictic certainty. But neither will he ever be in a position to prove his opinion. Rather, we will always have a greater right to assume a faculty of knowledge as one of the realities in the original being. Yet not a faculty like the one met with in men; but rather a faculty of a wholly different kind. We cannot in the least think how a reality could be in an effect without already being in its cause. How could beings with understanding be derived from an original source which is dead and without a faculty of knowledge? We do not have the least concept of the way in which one reality could produce other realities without being in any way similar to them. From what could the human faculty of knowledge be derived, if not from such a faculty in the original being?

Thus we see that speculative reason not only presents no obstacle to our assuming a faculty of knowledge in a highest being, but it even urges us to assume it, since otherwise we would have to search for another reality in this being as the cause of our faculty of knowledge. But this would have to be some reality of which we have no concept at all. Not only would it have to remain completely unknown to us, but there would also be no ground at all from which it could be thought.

But why should we take refuge in such an unknown, incomprehensible reality of God, when we can much more easily account for our faculty of knowledge by deriving it from the supreme intelligence of the highest original being? Who can deny that the faculty of knowledge is in general a reality and hence should also be attributed to a most real being? Hence God has a faculty of knowledge. But all the limitations found in our faculty of knowledge must be carefully separated out if we are to think of such a faculty in the highest being. Hence:

First: God's faculty of knowledge is not sensible, but rather *pure understanding*. We should exclude all sensibility from an *ente originario* because as an *ens independens* it cannot be affected by any object. But sensible knowledge is obtained from objects which have some influence on us. In the case of God, there can be no influence on him by any object, and therefore no sensible knowledge. In an original being, all knowledge must necessarily flow from a pure understanding not affected by any representation of sense. Hence it is not because sensible representations are obscure that they cannot be ascribed to God (as is commonly said). For we often find that a representation of sense is much clearer than certain modes of knowledge gained through the understanding. Instead, everything sensible must be removed from God because, as we have shown above, it is impossible for objects to influence an independent being.

Second: God's understanding is *intuitive*. It is a limitation of our understanding that we can argue to the particular only from the universal. This limitation cannot in any way be ascribed to a most real being. Such a being must rather intuit all things immediately through its understanding, and know everything at once. We are unable to form any concept of such an intuitive understanding, because *we* can only intuit by means of the senses. But it follows from God's supreme reality and originality that such an understanding must be present in him.

Third: God knows everything *a priori*. We can only know a few things without prior sensible intuition. Indeed, it is impossible in the case of any thing of which we are not ourselves the author. For instance, we can represent a garden we have planned a priori in our thought, before it actually exists. But this is not possible for things which lie outside our sphere of operation.

The original being is the ground of everything possible. Everything existing is dependent on it and derives from it. Hence it must know every possibility a priori, even before it exists.

God knows all things by knowing himself as the ground of all possibility. This is what has been called *theologia archetypa* or *exemplaris*, as we have mentioned previously.[32] Thus God has no empirical knowledge, because this would be a contradiction in an independent, original being.

We men know very little a priori, and have our senses to thank for nearly all our knowledge. Through experience we know only appearances, the *modum phaenomenon* or *sensibilem*, but not the *modum noumenon* or *intelligibilem*, not things as they are in themselves. This is shown at large in the theory of being (ontology). God knows all things as they are in themselves a priori and immediately through an intuitive understanding. For he is the being of all beings and every possibility has its ground in him. If we were to flatter ourselves so much as to claim that we know the *modum noumenon*, then we would have to be in community with God so as to participate immediately in the divine ideas, which are the authors of all things in themselves. To expect this in the present life is the business of mystics and theosophists. Thus arises the mystical self-annihilation of China, Tibet, and India, in which one is under the delusion that he will finally be dissolved in the Godhead. Fundamentally Spinozism could just as well be called a great fanaticism as a form of atheism. For of God, the one substance, Spinoza affirms two predicates: extension and thought. Every soul, he says, is only a modification of God's thought, and every body is a modification of his extension. Thus Spinoza assumed that everything existing could be found in God. But by making this assumption he fell into crude contradictions. For if only a single substance exists, then either I must be this substance, and consequently I must be God (but this contradicts my dependency); or else I am an accident (but this contradicts the concept of my ego, in which I think myself as an ultimate subject which is not the predicate of any other being).

Attention, abstraction, reflection, and comparison are only aids to a discursive understanding. Hence they cannot be thought in God. God has no *conceptus*, but only *intuitus*; and

32. "The knowledge of God is THEOLOGY IN THE WIDER SENSE. That theology by which God knows himself is EXEMPLARY THEOLOGY (*Theologia exemplaris*) (*archetypos*)" (Baumgarten, *Metaphysica*, §866).

so his understanding knows immediately every object as it is in itself. On the other hand, every concept is something mediate and originates from some universal characteristic. But an understanding which knows everything immediately, an intuitive understanding, has no need of reason. For reason is only a characteristic of the limits of an understanding and provides it with concepts. But an understanding which receives concepts through itself has no need of reason. Thus the expression *reason* is beneath the dignity of the divine nature. This concept should be wholly left out of the most real being, and it would be better to ascribe to it only an intuitive understanding as the highest perfection of knowledge. In this life we have no concept of such an immediate intuition of the understanding. But it can neither be denied nor demonstrated that a separated soul, as an intelligence, might contain a similar intuition in place of sensibility, so as to know things in themselves in their divine ideas.

Baumgarten divides God's knowledge into: (1) *scientiam simplicis intelligentiae* [knowledge of simple intellect], (2) *scientiam liberam* [free knowledge], and (3) *scientiam mediam* [middle knowledge].[33] As for the expression *scientific knowledge* (*scientia*), it is improper to apply it to God. For in God we should

33. "God knows (*scit*) every determination of every thing, insofar as mere possibility pertains to it. This is KNOWLEDGE OF SIMPLE INTELLECT (*Scientia Simplicis Intelligentiae*). . . . God knows every determination of what is actual in (1) this world, and this is his FREE KNOWLEDGE (*Scientia Libera*) (or vision) of (a) the past (the *divine memory*), (b) the present (*knowledge by vision*), and (c) the future (*foreknowledge*). . . . God knows every determination of what is actual in (2) other [possible] worlds, which is his MIDDLE KNOWLEDGE (*Scientia Media*)" (Baumgarten, *Metaphysica*, §§874–876). The distinctions drawn here were first devised by the sixteenth-century Jesuit theologian Luis de Molina. According to Molina, God knows everything that is possible through his "knowledge of simple intellect" and everything absolutely existing through his "knowledge of vision." But God also knows, prior to any absolute decree on his part, what he will decree concerning future contingents. This knowledge, falling midway between knowledge of mere possibles and knowledge of absolute existents, is what Molina calls God's "middle knowledge." Molina's purpose, of course, is to show how God's infallible foreknowledge can be reconciled with real contingency, and in particular with human free choice. Kant presently criticizes Baumgarten on the ground that there is no difference between "knowledge of simple intellect" and "middle knowledge," since both consist simply in God's knowledge of possible worlds other than the actual one. Baumgarten, however, seems to want to treat God's "middle knowledge" not as a knowledge of possible things generally, but as a kind of knowledge of actual things (viz. of

make no distinction between *scientific knowledge*, *belief*, and *opinion*, because all his knowledge is intuitive and thus excludes opinion. Thus it is not necessary to apply the anthropomorphic term *science* to God's knowledge. It is better to call it simply *knowledge*. And Baumgarten's division itself will hardly hold water if we try to think of it in relation to God. For the term *scientia simplicis intelligentiae* is understood by Baumgarten to mean the knowledge of everything possible, while *scientia libera* means the knowledge of everything actual. But with respect to God there is no distinction between the possible and the actual. For a complete knowledge of the possible is simultaneously a knowledge of the actual. The actual is already included within the possible, since what is actual must also be possible, for otherwise it would not be actual.

Thus if God is thinking of everything possible, he is already thinking of everything actual. So the distinction between *scientia simplicis intelligentiae* and *scientia libera* is only to be found in *our* human representation of God's knowledge, and not in this knowledge itself. That is, we represent to ourselves that in knowing his own essence (*simplex intelligentia*) God must also know everything possible, since he is the ground of all possibilities. Thus we derive the knowledge of all possibilities from his nature, and call it *cognitionem simplicis intelligentiae*.

We think of *scientia libera* as God's knowledge of the actual, insofar as he is simultaneously conscious of his free choice of things. For either all things are actual by the necessity of God's nature (which would be the principle of *emanation*); or else they exist through his will (which would be the system of *creation*). We think of a *scientiam liberam* in God to the extent that in his knowledge of everything possible, God is at the same time conscious in his free will of those possible things which he has made actual. Hence this representation is grounded on the system of creation, according to which God is the author of all things through his will. But the same account also follows from the

---

their nonactualized possibilities), and to found the distinction on this difference. But it seems that "middle knowledge" means something different for Baumgarten from what it did for Molina. For instead of being knowledge of future contingent actualities, it seems to be knowledge only of nonactualized possibilities.

principle of emanation. For since everything existing is actual through the necessity of the divine nature, God must be conscious of all things. But he is not conscious of them insofar as he is conscious of his choice of things; rather, he is conscious of them insofar as he is conscious of his own nature as a cause of all things. All of God's knowledge is grounded on his being an *ens entium*, an independent original being. For if God were not the cause of things, then either he would not know them at all (because there would be nothing in his nature which could acquaint him with things external to him); or else things would have to have some influence on him in order to give him a characteristic of their existence. But in that case, God would have to have sensible knowledge of things. Consequently, he would have to be *passibilis*, which contradicts his independence as an *entis originarii*. If God is thus able to know things apart from sensibility, he cannot know them except by being conscious of himself as the cause of everything. Thus the divine knowledge of all things is nothing but the knowledge God has of himself as an effective power.

Baumgarten further divides *scientiam liberam* into (1) *recordationem* [memory], (2) *scientiam visionis* [knowledge by vision], and (3) *praescientiam* [foreknowledge]. This division is again expressed according to human representations and cannot be thought in the divine knowledge itself. For God, the unchangeable, nothing is past or future, since he does not exist in time. He knows everything simultaneously, whether it is present to our representation or not. If God knows everything, he also knows our free actions, even those which we will perform at a future time. But the freedom of our actions is not canceled or limited by the fact that God foresees them. For he simultaneously foresees the whole nexus in which these actions are comprehended, including the motives for which we do them and the intentions we strive to realize by means of them. But if God foresees all this, he still does not at all predetermine that it must happen as it does. God's foreknowledge does not make our future actions necessary, as some have erroneously believed. God sees only that this or that action will take place. Besides, the concept of foreseeing is anthropomorphic and hence may not be thought in God himself. Therefore, there is not the least further difficulty in representing the manner in which God knows the future free actions of men. Insight into the one is just as necessary for our reason as insight into the other.

It is also wholly useless to distinguish the so-called *scientia media*, or knowledge of what could have happened in possible worlds other than the present actual one. For if God knows everything possible, then he knows it as much in itself as *in nexu*, and consequently in just this way he knows every possible world as a whole.

A mode of knowledge is *free* if the object itself depends on this knowledge. Hence our knowledge is not free, because the objects themselves are *given*, and our knowledge of objects depends on this. Our knowledge must adjust itself to the constitution of objects. God's knowledge, on the other hand, is free, because the existence of the world depends on it. The freedom of God's knowledge presupposes that God is the cause of the world through freedom, or the author of the world.

All error presupposes illusion and something misleading. It is not merely a lack of knowledge, for this would only be ignorance. Rather, error is a consequence of some positive obstacle to the truth. Now God knows nothing *a posteriori*. No object can have any influence on him, because he is independent, the original being, and consequently *impassibilis*. But just because no object can influence God, none can deceive him. God is therefore *infallibilis*. Proofs like this one, which are derived from certain predicates belonging to God, are always better than proofs derived merely from the concept of an *entis realissimi*.[34] For in the latter case it is often difficult to decide whether something is in fact a pure reality.

Baumgarten calls the *scientiam visionis* or *scientiam liberam* an *analogon modi* [modal analogue], as if the knowledge of an actual thing contained more than the knowledge of something possible.[35] But the difference between a thing's being at first possi-

34. Baumgarten (*Metaphysica*, §879) appears to infer God's infallibility simply from the fact that the possibility of error would be a defect.

35. "God's free knowledge is one of his perfections. And since he is an absolutely necessary being, this knowledge in him must be most true. Yet God

ble and then its becoming actual is only a distinction with respect to temporal relationships, and does not pertain to God at all.

Baumgarten now goes on to another property of God, the divine *wisdom*.[36] But this is premature, because wisdom presupposes a faculty of desire, and this faculty has not yet been proven in God. For as *summa intelligentia*, God has three predicates drawn from psychology which have been ascribed to him: (1) knowledge, (2) pleasure and pain,[37] and (3) a faculty of desire. For the sake of economy, then, we will postpone our

---

causes this world to exist such a way that it is in and for itself contingent. For this reason it is absolutely necessary that [God's free knowledge] be necessary only hypothetically. Therefore, God's free knowledge is a modal analogue (*analogon modi*)" (Baumgarten, *Metaphysica*, §881). Kant seems entirely to miss the point of the difficulty Baumgarten raises here. The actual world is supposed to be created by God freely, and so its existence is contingent. But God's knowledge of this world as the actual world (his "free knowledge"), like all the properties of an absolutely necessary being, is supposed to belong to him necessarily. Yet how is this possible? For if a proposition (i.e. "Such and such possible world is the actual world") is only contingently true, how can it be a necessary truth that anyone (even God) should know that this proposition is true? Baumgarten's attempt to solve the problem by appealing to a special case of the theory of analogy seems confused and unacceptable. For "modal analogues" are only hypothetical necessities in finite things which bear some *resemblance* to absolute necessities in God (cf. Baumgarten, *Metaphysica*, §827). Now no doubt the existence of the actual world *is* hypothetically necessary (contingent on God's choice of the best), and God's knowledge of it *is* supposed to be absolutely necessary. But this is not a case of the one necessity resembling the other; it is rather a case (apparently) of an absolute necessity being contingent on a hypothetical necessity (which is of course absurd). Perhaps a better solution would be this: If such and such possible world is the actual world, then it is so only contingently, and so it cannot be a necessary truth about God (or one of his genuine properties) that he knows "Such and such world is the actual world." But by itself, this is no problem. For instance, it is only contingently true that St. Thomas offered five proofs for God's existence. Hence it is not a necessary truth about God (or one of his genuine properties) that St. Thomas offered five proofs for his existence. Yet whatever possible world happens (contingently) to be the actual world, it is a necessary truth about God (and one of his genuine properties) that his knowledge about the actual world is accurate. And this can be a necessary truth even if the truths thus known are only contingent truths.

36. Kant's objection here would seem to be well taken, to the extent that Baumgarten (like Kant) explicitly includes in wisdom (*sapientia*) the ability to perceive final ends (*Sapientia Generatim*), particular ends (*Sapientia Speciatim*) and means to them (*Prudentia*) (*Metaphysica*, §882).

37. Pleasure = *Lust*. Pain = *Unlust*. The terms translate Baumgarten's *voluptas* and *taedium*, respectively (cf. *Metaphysica*, §655).

treatment of God's wisdom. But so as not to leave Baumgarten's order behind altogether, we will now deal with it provisionally.

Any being which has knowledge must have the following two properties in its knowledge:

(1) *Theoretical* perfection of its knowledge. This property would belong to it insofar as it is either ordinary knowledge or science. Yet neither of these applies to God, but both apply to men only. For ordinary knowledge is an aggregate, while science is a system of knowledge. Both contain a collection of knowledge, the only distinction being that in the one knowledge is just accumulated without being ordered by any principle, whereas in the other it is bound up in common as a unity. The theoretical perfection of God's knowledge is called *omniscience*.

(2) *Practical* perfection of its knowledge. This includes the following three properties: (a) Skill, which is perfection in knowing how to choose the means to arbitrary ends; (b) Prudence, which is knowledge of the means to given ends insofar as these means are not fully in my power. The means in question are rational beings. Hence prudence is nothing but a skill in making use of freely acting beings for given ends. (c) Wisdom, which is perfection in knowing how to derive each end from the system of all ends. Contentment rests on the unity of ends.

It can easily be seen that the first two kinds of perfection in knowledge (skill and prudence) cannot be predicated of God, because they involve too great a similarity to what is human, and what is real in them is already contained in omniscience. How, for instance, is prudence to be ascribed to God? For he has the full perfection of power, and consequently no end can ever be given whose means are not fully in his power. It is beneath the dignity of the divine nature to think of God as skillful or prudent. But wisdom, properly understood, can apply only to a being of the highest perfection. For who else knows the system of all ends, and who else is in a position to derive every end from it? If we predicate wisdom of men, then this can mean no more than the position of all one's ends in harmony with morality. For morality has the object of considering how each end might be posited in harmony with the idea of a whole composed of all ends, and it judges every action according to common rules.

Insofar as our knowledge of human actions is derived from the principle of a possible system of all ends, it can be called human wisdom. Hence we are even able to give an example *in concreto* of a highest understanding which infers from the whole to the particular. This example is our moral conduct. For in it we determine the value of each end by means of an idea of the whole composed of all ends. But in our concept of happiness, we have no concept of the whole. Rather, we put it together from parts. And just for this reason, we cannot arrange our actions according to an idea of happiness, because a whole of this sort cannot be thought by us.

But man does have an idea of a whole composed of *all* ends, even though he never fully attains to this idea, and thus is not himself wise. In this way the divine wisdom is distinguished from human wisdom not only in quantity but also in quality, just as God's absolute necessity is distinguished from the existence of all other things.

God's wisdom also consists in the agreement of divine choice with itself. A plan involving selection,[38] which in its execution would produce collisions and thus require exceptions, could not be the most perfect plan. Hence God's plan for the arrangement of nature has to be conjoined with the divine will as a whole. And this complete unity in the choice of means to his ends is a property of God's wisdom. But we must postpone further discussion of this subject until after our treatment of the divine will, where it really belongs.

Baumgarten also deals with God's *omniscience*, and treats it as a property distinct from the divine knowledge.[39] But we cannot take any specific note of God's scientific knowledge, as if to distinguish it from belief, opinion and conjecture. For the latter do not apply to God at all, since he knows everything. It is just for this reason that his knowledge is scientific knowledge; for scien-

38. Choice = *Wahl*. Selection = *Auswahl*.

39. "Omniscience is the knowledge of everything (*scientia omnium*)" (Baumgarten, *Metaphysica*, §889). Baumgarten attributed knowledge (*scientia*) to God back in section 873.

tific knowledge follows from an all-sufficiency of knowledge. Just because we do not always know things completely, our knowledge is often not scientific knowledge but belief. But God's complete knowledge of everything is his omniscience.

To conclude our treatment of the divine knowledge, we will add a note concerning the Platonic idea. The term *idea* properly signifies a *simulacrum*, and thus in human philosophy it signifies a concept of reason, insofar as no possible experience can ever be adequate to it. Plato thought of the divine ideas as the archetypes of things. These things are arranged according to the archetypes, but they are never posited as adequate to the divine idea itself. God's idea of man, for instance, regarded as an archetype, would be the most perfect idea of the most perfect man. Particular individuals, actual men, are formed according to this idea, but they never fully correspond to it.

Plato was subsequently accused of treating these ideas in God as pure substances. And in the second century there finally emerged a so-called eclectic sect which dreamed of the possibility of participating in the divine ideas. The whole of mystic theosophy is based on this, and thus it is fundamentally nothing but a corrupt Platonic philosophy.

[God's Will]

We have now dealt with the first of God's predicates drawn from psychology, the faculty of knowledge or understanding. Baumgarten now proceeds to discuss the *will* of God,[40] which is a practical perfection, just as the understanding is a theoretical perfection. Here many difficulties show themselves right away at the beginning, as soon as we ask: Does God have a faculty of desire? And how is it constituted? All desires are either immanent or transient. That is, either they refer to the very thing which has them and remains in this thing, or else they refer to something which is external to the thing. But neither of these alternatives can be thought in a being of all beings. In the first place, an all-sufficient being cannot have immanent desires, simply because he is all-sufficient. For every desire always con-

40. Part IV, Section III (§§890–925) of Baumgarten's *Metaphysica* deals with the *Voluntas Dei*.

cerns something possible and future. But since God has all perfections actually, there is nothing left over for him to desire as a future possibility. But neither can God be represented as desiring something external to him. For then he would need the existence of other things in order to fulfill the consciousness of his own existence. But this goes against the concept of an *entis realissimi*. Thus the big question is: How can we think of a most perfect being as having desires? To answer this question, let us undertake the following investigations. The powers of our mind are: (1) *knowledge*; (2) the feeling of *pleasure* and *pain*, or better, since the word *feeling* appears to imply something sensible, the faculty of *well-pleasedness* and *displeasure*;[41] and (3) the faculty of *desire*.

There are only a few beings which have a faculty of representation. If a being's representations can become the cause of the objects of representation (or of their actuality), then the being is called a *living* being. Hence a faculty of desire is the causality of the faculty of representation with respect to the actuality of its objects. The will is the faculty of ends.

Well-pleasedness cannot consist in the consciousness of perfection, as Baumgarten defines it, because perfection is the harmony of a manifold in a unity.[42] But here I do not want to know what it is that I take pleasure in, I rather want to know what

41. Well-pleasedness = *Wohlgefallenheit*. Displeasure = *Missfallenheit*. The former translates Baumgarten's *complacientia* and the latter his *displacientia*. The term *Wohlgefallenheit* also has biblical connotations (e.g. "Thou art my beloved Son; in thee I am well pleased" [Luke 3:22]). Baumgarten (*Metaphysica*, §891), like Kant, insists that pleasure (*Lust, voluptas*) and pain (*Unlust, taedium*) do not pertain to God, since they imply sensible appetites and aversions. The difference between pleasure and well-pleasedness (and between pain and displeasure) seems to consist solely in the fact that the former term implies that the origin of the feeling is sensible, whereas the latter term does not necessarily imply this. Hence well-pleasedness and displeasure can be predicated of God, whereas pleasure and pain cannot.

42. Baumgarten (*Metaphysica*, §655) defines well-pleasedness as "a state of the soul occasioned by the intuition of perfection." Kant's real reason for objecting to this definition is his belief that the relation between pleasure and any object (or state of affairs represented as a possible effect of action) is always a contingent one, knowable only through experience. This is his reason for denying that any material practical principle (or principle presupposing a desired end as motive for the will) could ever qualify as an a priori practical law or categorical imperative (cf. *Critique of Practical Reason, Gesammelte Schriften*, vol. 5,

pleasure itself is. Now pleasure itself does not consist in the relation of my representations to their objects, it consists rather in the relation of representations to the subject insofar as these representations determine the subject to actualize the object. Insofar as a representation is the cause of the actuality of its object, it is called a *faculty of desire*. But insofar as it first determines the subject to the desire, it is called *pleasure*. Thus it can obviously be seen that pleasure precedes desire.[43] Well-pleasedness with one's own existence, when this existence is dependent, is called *happiness*. Thus happiness is my contentment with my own

---

p. 21, and *Foundations of the Metaphysic of Morals, Gesammelte Schriften*, vol. 4, p. 443–444). Baumgarten, like Wolff, held the stoic view that perfection of character was an end desirable a priori which could serve as the ground of moral volition. In this context, however, Kant's objection seems to be somewhat misplaced. For here the subject is not man's sensible faculty of pleasure and pain, but God's faculty of well-pleasedness and displeasure. And Kant surely agrees that the connection between God's well-pleasedness and his consciousness of perfection is an a priori one.

43. The theory of desire expressed in this passage is once again more fitting to the finite human will than to the will of God. The theory itself is taken over in part from the rationalists and is in certain respects confusing and counterintuitive. The faculty of desire, according to Kant, is determined (*bestimmt*) to actualize some object (or end) insofar as (1) the end is represented (*vorgestellt*) by the subject and (2) there is some motive or reason (*Bewegungsgrund, Bestimmungsgrund*) which determines or causes the subject to actualize the object (or end) thus represented. Now *one* way in which this happens is when the representation of this end stands in a certain positive relation to the subject, that is, "agrees" with his sensitive faculties. Such a relation of agreement between a representation and the subject is what Kant calls pleasure (*Lust*). A representation, when accompanied by this feeling of pleasure, is capable of determining (i.e. motivating or causing) the subject to actualize the end represented. Hence in such cases pleasure (causally) *precedes* desire and is in fact its efficient cause. This means that pleasure, in Kant's use of the term, is *not* what we feel when we get what we desire; it is rather what we feel when we imagine (or represent) what we desire, before we have set about getting it. The feeling of *satisfaction* we get from the possession (or actualization) of what we desire when we actually have it is something quite distinct from "pleasure" in this sense. (In the *Critique of Practical Reason*, Kant calls the satisfaction in our object attained "agreeableness" [*Annehmlichkeit*], and he describes pleasure [*Lust*] as an "expected agreeableness" [*Gesammelte Schriften*, vol. 5, pp. 22–23]). Pleasure (or its opposite, pain) of course is for Kant only one possible sort of motive for the will, and in fact all actions motivated by pleasure or pain in some represented state of affairs are without exception heteronomous and devoid of moral worth. Only actions motivated not by pleasure in an object but by pure reason, the moral law, the legislative form of one's maxim or duty (Kant's various names for the same motive) are autonomous and morally good.

dependent existence. But a complete well-pleasedness with one's own independent existence is called *acquiescentia in semetipso* or self-sufficiency (*beatitudo*). This blessedness of a being consists therefore in a well-pleasedness in his own existence apart from any need, and thus it belongs only to God; for he alone is independent. Hence if the will of God has to be represented as the will of a self-sufficient being, then it follows that before treating of the divine will, it will be necessary first to consider the faculty of the object of well-pleasedness and displeasure, and then also the self-sufficiency of God. This attempt is new; but it is founded on the natural sequence of ideas, according to which something must be discussed first if the matter at hand cannot be clearly known without it. Thus in order to answer the main question as to the manner in which a faculty of desire could be found in a most real being and how this faculty would have to be constituted, we must first deal with God's faculty of pleasure and pain, and with his blessedness.

If there is to be a conjunction of the divine understanding with volition, then it must be shown how a self-sufficient being could be the cause of something external to itself. For God's will is derived from the fact that he is supposed to be the creator of the world. We see very well that things in the world can be the cause of something else. Yet this quality does not refer to the things themselves; it refers rather only to their determinations: not to their substance, but only to their form. It follows that the causality by which God is supposed to be the author of the world must be of a wholly different kind. For it is impossible to think of God's causality, his faculty of actualizing things external to himself, as anything different from his understanding. Or in other words, a being which is self-sufficient can only become the cause of things external to itself by means of its understanding. And it is just this causality of God's understanding, his actualization of the objects of his representation, which is called will. The causality of the highest being as regards the world, or the will through which he makes it, rests on his highest understanding, and cannot rest on anything else. We can think of the opposite of an understanding, of a blindly working eternal root of all things, a *natura bruta*. But how can the divine will be found in this causality? Without an understanding, it would have no faculty at all for referring itself, its own subject, to something else, or for representing something external to itself. And yet it is only under this one condition that anything can be the cause of other things external to itself. From this it follows that an all-sufficient being can produce things external to itself only through will, and not through the necessity of its nature. The self-sufficiency of God, connected to his understanding, is all-sufficiency. For in knowing himself, he knows everything possible which is contained in him as its ground. The well-pleasedness of a being with itself as a possible ground for the production of things is what determines its causality.

The same thing can be expressed in other words by saying that the cause of God's will consists in the fact that despite his highest self-contentment, things external to him are to exist insofar as he is conscious of himself as an all-sufficient being. God knows himself by means of his highest understanding as the all-sufficient ground of everything possible. He is most well-pleased with his unlimited faculty as regards all possible things, and it is just this well-pleasedness with himself which causes him to actualize these possibilities. Hence it is just this which is God's desire to produce things external to himself. The product of such a will must be the greatest whole of everything possible, that is, the *summum bonum finitum*, the most perfect world.

If we represent God's will in this manner, which is suitable to the highest being, then all the usual objections to the possibility of volition in a self-sufficient being will collapse. It is said, for instance, that a being which desires something external to itself can only be contented if what it desires actually exists. Hence volition, or the desire for something, presupposes that the well-pleasedness or contentment of a being with such desires can only be complete through the existence of other things. And indeed it is true of every created being that the desire for something always presupposes a need, and it is because of this need that I desire it. But why is this? It is simply because no creature is all-sufficient, and so each one always has need of many things. Just for this reason it always reaches a higher degree of self-contentment when what it desires is produced. But in a being which is independent and thus self-sufficient as well, the ground of its volition and desire that things external to itself should exist is just that it knows its own faculty for actualizing things external to itself.

Hence according to pure reason, we see that a faculty of desire and volition may be found in a self-sufficient being. In fact, it is impossible to think of a being which combines the highest self-contentment with a supreme understanding, unless we also think in it a causality as regards the objects of its representations. Of course we must stay away from an anthropomorphic concept of volition at this point. For otherwise vain contradictions will result instead of agreement.

Now before we proceed to our proper treatment of the divine will, we must first consider an introduction to it borrowed from physicotheology.

Third Section: Physicotheology

[The Physicotheological Proof]

The question is: From the purposive order of nature can one infer an intelligent author of this order? In his *Dialogues*, Hume raises an objection to this inference which is by no means weak. He says that even assuming that there is a supreme cause which has brought about all the order in nature through understanding and freedom, we still cannot comprehend how this supreme intelligence could have all the perfections necessary to produce such a harmony, or where all these excellences in such a being might come from. We can no more comprehend this, he says, than we can comprehend the origin of the perfections of the world apart from the presupposition of an intelligent author.[44]

44. Kant evidently has in mind Philo's objection to Cleanthes' natural theology: "How therefore shall we satisfy ourselves concerning the cause of that Being, whom you suppose the Author of Nature, or, according to your system of anthropomorphism, the ideal world, into which you trace the material? Have we not the same reason to trace that ideal world into another ideal world, or new intelligent principle? But if we stop, and go no farther, why go so far? Why not stop at the material world? How can we satisfy ourselves without going on *in infinitum*? And after all, what satisfaction is there in that infinite progression?"

We can feel the full force of Hume's objection only after we have come to see that it is quite impossible for us either to assert that a supreme original being is absolutely necessary, or to know the cause of God's existence itself. For the question: Where do all the perfections in God come from? is an unanswerable one.

On the other hand, we have already shown that we can have no insight through our reason into the existence of a being whose nonexistence is impossible. Or in a word, we have no insight into an existence which is absolutely necessary. And yet our reason urges us on to such a being as a *hypothesis* which is subjectively necessary for us to assume, because otherwise we could provide no ground for the possibility of anything in general. But if it is a true need of our speculative reason to assume a God, nevertheless from the fact that men cannot prove this apodictically nothing follows except that such a proof transcends our faculty of reason. But as regards Hume's objection, it is mistaken despite its apparent strength. For let us now compare two hypotheses. The first is: A supremely perfect being is the author of the world through its understanding. And the second hypothesis is: A blindly working eternal nature is the cause of all the purposiveness and order in the world. Now let us see whether we are able to assume this latter hypothesis. Can we think without contradiction that the purposiveness, beauty, and harmony of the world have arisen from a *natura bruta*? These things obviously have to be predicates of an understanding. So how could nature, simply of itself, arrange the various things in harmony with its determinate final aims, using so many united means? Everywhere in the world we find a chain of ef-

---

(Hume, *Dialogues*, Part IV, p. 34). But Kant seems not to use the argument in the sense it was meant. Philo was asking for an explanation of God's ideas, whereas Kant is speaking about God's perfections. More importantly, Philo intends the argument to show that it is pointless to hypothesize a divine intelligence as cause of the world's order, since the qualities of this intelligence are even more inexplicable than the qualities of nature they are meant to explain. Kant, however, is using the argument to support the perplexing unanswerability (but by no means the pointlessness) of the question: What is the ground of God's perfections? Yet Kant clearly understood the import of Philo's argument, as is shown by his rejection in the next paragraph of a *natura bruta* as cause of natural purposiveness.

fects and causes, of ends and means, of regularity in the coming to be and perishing of things. How could this whole, just of itself, come to be in its present state? Or how could merely a blind all-powerful nature be the cause of it?

Purposiveness in the effects always presupposes understanding in the cause. Or what cooperation of blind accidents could produce a moth, with its purposive structure? Hume says that a mere fecundity is certainly in a position to produce harmony in its effects.[45] We can see this right now in the way things come to be in the world. We ourselves, as intelligent beings, are generated by our parents through the senses, and not through understanding. Very well; but what about the whole of all things, the totality of the world? Is it therefore generated by some fertile cause? What a sophistry!

Could a being have understanding when, like the world, it is a composite of true substances? Is it possible for us to think of an understanding which is distributed? It is certainly more comprehensible to us if we assume that a highest understanding and will have planned and carried out all the purposive arrangements of the world, rather than supposing that a fertile cause without understanding generated all this from the necessity of its nature. The latter supposition cannot even be thought without contradiction. For assuming that we think of nature as such a blindly working original being, it would never have had the capacity to relate itself to subjects, to things outside it. But then how could it have the causality or the capacity to actualize things outside it, and indeed things which are to agree with a plan? But if the things of the world are generated simply through fertility, then what is generated are only the *forms* of things. As regards their first origin, the things themselves which are already contained in the senses could only have been produced by some being with freedom and understanding. But if on the contrary we do assume a highest intelligence which through its will has caused the whole of creation, then it is not at all incomprehensible to me how purposive order could be found in nature, since I derive it from a supreme understanding. And if we ask

45. Philo employs this idea throughout Parts VI and VII of Hume's *Dialogues*.

how this supreme being has sufficient perfections and *where* it gets them, the answer can only be that they follow from its absolute necessity. Of course on account of the limits of my reason I really have no insight into such a necessity, but for just the same reason I also cannot deny it.

[The Divine Will]

Following this preliminary introduction, we will now turn to our real treatment of the divine will, and in it we will follow the order of Baumgarten's paragraphs. Baumgarten first talks about the fact that God's faculty of desire cannot be sensible.[46] This follows because God, as an *ens originarium independens*, cannot be affected by objects. But we have already given a detailed treatment of this point, and also of Baumgarten's discussion of the *acquiescentia Dei in semetipso*.[47] But if we ask what the divine will is, we can answer: it is the divine understanding determining God's activity to the production of the objects he represents. In men, well-pleasedness is pleasure in an object. Thus, for instance, I can be well-pleased with a house, even if I can only see the plans. But well-pleasedness in the *existence* of an object is called *interest*.[48] But I cannot predicate either one of God. He

46. "God's well-pleasedness and displeasure are not . . . pleasure or pain, nor does he have sensitive appetites or aversions" (Baumgarten, *Metaphysica*, §891).

47. "Because God intuits himself most distinctly as the good and the supreme holiness . . . this acquiescence of God in himself is the exemplary theology, and the greatest delight" (Baumgarten, *Metaphysica*, §892).

48. Kant's idea here seems to be this: I can experience pleasure (or well-pleasedness) in relation to a representation in two ways. First, I can take pleasure just in contemplating the representation, whether or not the object represented has ever existed or will ever exist. The mere plans of a house, to cite Kant's example, may please me without my considering whether they are the plans of an existing house, or of one which will ever exist. On the other hand, my pleasure in a representation may be conditional on my representing the object as something actually existing (presumably in the future, if this pleasure is to motivate me to actualize the object). In this second case, my pleasure is called *interest*. Thus, for instance, I may take pleasure in the plans of a house only insofar as I represent the house as something actually to be built for me to live in. As mere plans, without the thought of my prospective enjoyment of the house projected in them, they may leave me cold. Here my pleasure in the representation of the house is an *interested* pleasure. The notion of disinterested pleasure, of course, was later to play a major role in Kant's aesthetic theory in the *Critique of Judgment*.

has no pleasure and no interest. For he is self-sufficient and has a complete self-contentment in his independent existence. God needs no thing external to him, and nothing outside him could increase his blessedness. Hence we can ascribe to God only an analogue of interest, that is, a similarity of relation. The relation of everything good in the world to the will of God is the same as the relation of a benevolent deed to the will of the being who does the deed for me, when this being from whom I receive the benevolence is happy and has no need of me. Beyond this, the nature of God's will is unknown. I know only that his will is pure goodness, and that is enough for me.

Thus the stoics thought of the ideal sage who feels no compassion for distress and yet whose greatest delight would be to remedy every distress. This ideal is not possible for me. For an incentive must be added to my knowledge of a good before I can actually will to produce the good. This is because my activity is limited, and thus if I am to apply my powers to the production of some good I must first judge whether in this way I am not exhausting faculties which might have produced some other good. In this case I need certain incentives to determine my powers to this or that good, since I do not have faculties sufficient for the actual production of everything I know to be good.

These incentives consist in certain subjective relations which must determine my well-pleasedness in choosing, subsequent to the determination of my well-pleasedness in judging, or my knowledge of the good. If this subjective relation were removed, then my choice of the good would be canceled. But with God it is different. He has the greatest power combined with the highest understanding. Since his understanding knows his capacity to actualize the objects of his representation he is *eo ipso* determined to activity and to the production of the good, and indeed to the production of the greatest possible sum of all good. For God, the mere representation of a good is all that is required to actualize it. He does not need first to be motivated, and in his case there are no particular incentives. Indeed, no subjective relations are possible for him at all, because he is already all-sufficient in himself and has the highest blessedness. Hence if we talk about God's motives, nothing but the goodness of the object can be understood by it. And even here there are no subjective relations involved, as if God were out for praise or glory. For this would not be suitable to the dignity of a most blessed being. Rather, God knows through his understanding simultaneously both the possible good and his capacity to produce it. The reason why he actually does produce it is contained in his knowledge itself.

God's will is *free*. Freedom of the will is the capacity to determine oneself to actions independently of a *causis subjectis* [subjective cause] or sensuous impulses; or, the capacity to will a priori.[49] But since with us inclinations are the subjective conditions of self-contentment, the concept of human freedom is subject to many psychological difficulties. For man is a part of nature and he belongs to the world of sense. He is therefore also subject to the laws of appearances. All appearances are determined among themselves by certain laws, and it is just this determination of everything given in nature by universal laws which constitutes the mechanism of nature. Man, therefore, as a part of nature, is subject to this natural mechanism, or at least to a psychological mechanism. But how, then, can his actions be thought of as independent of the events given in nature. How can they be thought of as *free*? Certainly man is conscious of himself as an intellectual object. But even this consciousness has its psychological difficulties.

But here these difficulties do not concern us, for they do not apply to God at all. God is wholly distinct from the world and has no connection at all with space and time. Hence he is not subject to the laws of appearances and is in general not determined by anything. Consequently it is self-evident that his will is not determined by other things as incentives. Just as little is it possible for God to have an inclination to change his state; for he is self-sufficient. Hence if we want to think of the concept of divine freedom purified of every limitation, then it consists in nothing but the complete independence of God's will both from

49. Baumgarten (*Metaphysica*, §898) defines God's freedom of will as God's determining himself to act *pro lubitu*, that is, acting at his own discretion or whim (cf. Baumgarten, *Metaphysica*, §719). Kant obviously finds this definition inadequate and simply substitutes his own for it.

external things and from inner conditions. But if we have no need to fear that this concept of divine freedom will be exposed to any psychological difficulties (since these difficulties apply only to human freedom), on the other hand we still cannot avoid the defect that this concept cannot be represented *in concreto*, since all the conditions of sense have been done away with. Now just because this concept cannot be illustrated by an example, the suspicion might arise that the concept itself is obscure or even false. But once a concept has been introduced a priori with apodictic certainty, then we need fear no error, even if our incapacity and even our whole reason forbids us to set up a case of it *in concreto*. Now it can be proven that the divine will has to be entirely free, for otherwise God could not be an *ens originarium*, or in other words, could not be God. For as a *prima causa mundi*, his will must be independent of all things, because there is nothing which could serve as a motive to determine him to anything. Nor could any inclination toward something arise in him, since he possesses supreme self-contentment. To God belongs transcendental freedom, consisting in an absolute spontaneity, as well as practical freedom, or the independence of his will from any sensuous impulses. This absolute spontaneity of action cannot be proven at all in man; in fact, its possibility can never be known, because we men belong to the world and are affected by things. But in God it can be thought without the least difficulty. It is just the same with practical freedom, which must be presupposed in man if the whole of morality is not to be abolished.[50] Man acts according to the idea of freedom, he acts *as if* he were free, and *eo ipso* he is free. This capacity always to act according to reason must certainly be in God, since sensuous impulses are impossible in him. One might raise the objection that God cannot decide otherwise than he does, and so he does not act freely but out of the necessity of his nature. But man can always decide on something else. For instance, instead of being benevolent in this case, a man could be the opposite. But it is precisely this which is a lack of freedom in man, since he does not always act according to his reason. But

50. Abolished = *aufgehoben*.

in God it is not due to the necessity of his nature that he can decide only as he does. Rather it is true freedom in God that he decides only what is suitable to his highest understanding.

Fatalism predicates blind necessity of God, and thus contradicts the concept of a highest intelligence.[51] This perverted opinion does of course deserve to be called fatalism, just as we give the name *chance* to a blind accident. Fatalism arises when the blind necessity of nature is not distinguished from physical and practical necessity. Of course the fatalist appeals to examples where God is supposed to have acted only according to a necessity of nature. He might say, for instance, that God created the world so and so many years ago, but did nothing in the whole long eternity before that. According to the fatalist, this can only be explained by saying that God *had to* create the world just at that time. But how anthropomorphic this representation is! No years can be thought in God, and no time. He is not in time at all. And to limit his efficacy to the conditions of time is to think contrary to the concept of God.

Baumgarten appeals to a distinction in the divine volition between (1) *voluntas antecedentem* and (2) *voluntas consequentem*.[52] The *voluntas antecedens* refers to the object of my will according to universal concepts. For instance, a king wills to make his subjects happy simply because they are his subjects. The *voluntas consequens* refers to the object of my will in its thoroughgoing determination. For instance, a king wills to reward his subjects only insofar as they are worthy subjects. In both kinds of volition we must remove the human concept of time, according to which the will precedes what follows it. Only after this removal can we apply these kinds of volition to God, if we are to be faithful to the majesty of the highest being. This distinction in volition has a foundation in every rational being. But in God all succession must be omitted. In man the *voluntas antecedens* is a

51. "FATALISM, the proposition denying God's freedom, is an error" (Baumgarten, *Metaphysica*, §898).

52. "THE WILL OF GOD, insofar as it is the object of his free knowledge, or he desires the actual things of this universe, is called his CONSEQUENT WILL (*Voluntas Consequens*); insofar as it is turned toward universals and actual things in other [possible] universes, it is called his ANTECEDENT WILL (*Voluntas Antecedens*)" (Baumgarten, *Metaphysica*, §899).

provisional opinion of the will, but the *voluntas consequens* is final. In God, however, the *voluntas antecedens* is always already in the *decreto*. It refers only to what the object has in common with other things not willed by God.

It is clear that everything in the world happens according to a divine decree; for otherwise it would not exist. But now suppose we try to gain insight into the motives of the divine will; suppose we want to know what there was in the world that made God arrange it as he did, and to gain insight into the purposes of God's will. In this case we will of course find that God's will is *inscrutable*.[53] We may indeed make use of the analogy with a perfect will, and apply some of its aims to help us in particular cases. But such judgments must only be problematic, and we must not treat them as if they had apodictic certainty. It would be presumption, and a violation of God's holy right, to want to determine precisely that this or that is and had to be God's purpose in the production of a certain thing. In a few cases, God's wise will and his intentions are obvious. For instance, the whole structure of the human eye shows itself to be a wise means to the end of seeing. But it is not possible for our reason to decide whether in a certain thing we are meeting with an end in itself or only with a consequence of still higher ends. For the presupposition that everything in this world has its utility and its good aims would go much farther if it were a constitutive principle. But our previous observations cannot justify this. Yet even as a regulative principle it serves very well to extend our insight, and it can thus always be useful reason and never harmful to it. For if we approach the world with the assumption that it exhibits a thousand wise purposes of its creator, then we will be able to make a host of discoveries. In any case, the only error which can result from this is that of meeting with only a mechanical or physical connection (a *nexus effectivus*) where we expected a teleological one (a *nexus finalis*). In such a case we do miss one kind of unity, but we do not destroy the unity of rea-

53. "An INSCRUTABLE WILL is one whose impelling causes are incomprehensible. But the impelling causes of the divine will are most distinctly at God's own discretion (*ipsius lubitus*). For this reason [the will of God] is to God internally perfect, but to us incomprehensible" (Baumgarten, *Metaphysica*, §900).

son in its empirical employment. In a *nexu effectivo* the purpose is always last and the means is first. But in a *nexu finali* the aim always precedes the use of means. When a sick person, by means of medications, attains his end (health), this is an example of a *nexus effectivus*. But in the case of a *nexus finalis*, the sick person first sets himself the aim of becoming healthy before he applies the means.

In the case of God's will, we always know only the conditioned aim. For instance, if men are to exist they must see and hence their eyes must be arranged thus and not otherwise. But we never know God's final aim, for example, the reason why men exist in general. Of course we can be sure that men are ends, and not just the consequence of still higher ends. For the latter supposition would be degrading to rational beings. But this is the only case where we can be certain of such a thing. In the case of every other thing in the world, it is impossible to know whether its existence is a final aim of God, or only something necessary as a means to still higher ends.

The recognition that from the primary constitution of nature we can infer a supreme principle as a highest intelligence shows in general both the possibility and necessity of a physicotheology. Indeed, the principle that everything good and purposive comes from God can itself be termed a universal physicotheology. But if we find that a great deal of the order and perfection in nature has to be derived from the essence of things themselves according to universal laws, still in no way do we need to withdraw this order from God's supreme governance. Rather, these universal laws themselves always presuppose a principle connecting every possibility with every other. But to say that God's will is directed to ends is to ascribe a psychological predicate to it; and thus the nature of his will must remain incomprehensible to us, and its aims inscrutable.

The predicates of God's will dealt with thus far have been *ontological* ones. Those which remain to be discussed by us are its *moral* predicates.

Second Part: Moral Theology

First Section: The Moral Attributes of God

[Moral Faith in God]

The concept of God is not a natural concept, and it is not necessary from a psychological point of view. For in psychology and in the knowledge of nature I must never appeal directly to God whenever I perceive beauty and harmony. For this is a kind of lazy reason, which would gladly dispense with all further investigations into the natural causes of natural effects. Rather in such cases I must turn to a method which can further the cultivation of my reason, and I must seek out the proximate causes of such effects in nature itself. In this way I may come to know the universal laws according to which everything in the world proceeds. Earlier I saw that it was necessary for me to assume the hypothesis of a being containing in itself the ground of these universal laws. But even without this hypothesis I can still make great progress in physics by endeavoring to find all the intermediate causes. Physicotheology does not give me a determinate concept of God as an all-sufficient being; it only teaches me to know him as a very great and immeasurable being. But in this way I am not entirely satisfied regarding what I need to know of God. For I can always ask further whether perhaps another being is possible which might possess even more power and knowledge than the supreme principle of nature as I know it. But an indeterminate concept of God does not help me at all. Yet on the other hand, the concept of God is a *moral* concept, and *practically necessary*. For morality contains the conditions as regards the conduct of rational beings under which alone they can be worthy of happiness. These conditions, these duties, are apodictically certain. For they are grounded necessarily in the nature of a rational and free being. Only under these conditions can such a being become worthy of happiness. But if in the case of a creature who has conducted himself according to these eternal and immediate laws of nature, and who has thus become worthy of happiness, no state can be hoped for where he participates in this happiness; if no state of well-being follows his well-doing; then there would be a contradiction between morality and the course of nature. Yet experience and reason show us that in the present course of things the precise observation of all morally necessary duties is not always connected with well-being. Rather, the noblest honesty and righteousness is often misunderstood, despised, persecuted, and trodden under foot by vice. But then there must exist a being who rules the world according to reason and moral laws, and who has established, in the course of things to come, a state where the creature who has remained true to his nature and who has made himself worthy of happiness through morality will actually participate in this happiness. For otherwise all subjectively necessary duties which I as a rational being am responsible for performing will lose their objective reality. Why should I make myself worthy of happiness through morality if there is no being who can give me this happiness? Hence without God I would have to be either a visionary or a scoundrel. I would have to deny my own nature and its eternal moral laws. I would have to cease being a rational man.

Hence in moral theology the existence of God is not merely a hypothesis about contingent appearances, as it was in physicotheology. Instead, it is a necessary postulate for the incontrovertible laws of my own nature. For morality not only shows that we have need of God, but it also teaches us that he is already present in the nature of things and that the order of things leads to him. Of course first it must be firmly established that moral duties are necessarily grounded in the nature of everyone's reason and hence that they are binding on me with apodictic certainty. For if moral duties are based only on feelings, or on the prospect of happiness (so that I would become happy just by fulfilling them—not merely worthy of happiness, but through them an actual participant in happiness); then well-being would already exist in the present course of things as the effect of good conduct, and I would not need to count only on a happy state in the future or assume a being who could help me attain it. But no sufficient ground for morality is exhibited by Hume's principle when he tries to derive all of morality from particular moral feelings. And experience is against the proposition that virtue is already sufficiently rewarded in the present. Hence the duties of morality are apodictically certain, since they are set before me by my own reason. But if there were no God and no future world, there would be no incentives to act in accordance with these duties as a rational man.

Moreover, it is morality alone which gives me a *determinate* concept of God. It teaches me to know him as a being having every perfection. For God has to judge me according to the principles of morality, and decide whether I am deserving of happiness. And in case I am, he has to be able to let me actually participate in happiness. Such a God has to know even the most secret stirrings of my heart, because this chiefly determines the worth of my conduct. He must also have the whole of nature under his power, if he is to be able to order my future happiness in its course according to a plan. Finally, he has to arrange and direct the consequences of the different states of my existence. In short, he has to be *omniscient*, *omnipotent*, *eternal*, and *not in time*.

[God's Three Moral Attributes]

Any being who is to give objective reality to moral duties must possess without limit the moral perfections of *holiness*, *benevolence*, and *justice*. These three attributes constitute the whole moral concept of God. In God they belong together, but of course in our representation of them, they have to be distinguished from one another. Thus through morality we know God as a *holy lawgiver*, a *benevolent sustainer of the world*, and a *just judge*. We must give first thought to the holiness of the law, even though our interest commonly beguiles us so that we put God's benevolence above it. But a restrictive condition always precedes God's benevolence, under which men are to be deserving of this benevolence and of the happiness which flows from it. This condition is that they conduct themselves in accordance with the holy law. Hence this law must be presupposed if well-being is to follow upon it. A supreme principle of lawgiving must be altogether holy, and it must allow no vice or sin, or account them any less punishable than they are. For it should be an eternal norm for us, departing at no point from what is in accordance with morality.

Benevolence, once again, is a special idea, whose object is happiness just as the object of holiness can be nothing but strictly good conduct or the highest virtue.[1] Benevolence in and for itself is without limit, but it has to express itself in the apportionment of happiness according to the proportion of worthiness in the subject. And it is just this limitation of benevolence by holiness in apportioning happiness which is God's *justice*.[2] I must not think of a judge as benevolent, as relaxing and to some extent forgiving the holiness of the laws. For then he would not be a judge at all, since a judge must weigh and apportion happiness strictly according to the measure in which the subject has be-

1. "BENEVOLENCE (kindness) is the determination of the will to doing good to another . . . God wills to confer benefit on others. Therefore, he is kind" (Baumgarten, *Metaphysica*, §§903–904).

2. Baumgarten (*Metaphysica*, §906) agrees that "JUSTICE is benevolence proportionate to a person or spirit." But he does not reduce God's moral attributes to benevolence, holiness, and their combination justice, as Kant does. Baumgarten, indeed, treated God's supreme holiness much earlier in the *Metaphysica* and defined it simply as "the reality of a being by which all imperfections are denied in it" (*Metaphysica*, §828). Kant's treatment of God's moral attributes follows the pattern of triads used in the table of categories in the *Critique of Pure Reason*. Such a triad is composed of two contrasting concepts (in this case, benevolence, whose object is the happiness of creatures, and holiness, whose object is strictly good conduct) and a third in which the first two are somehow combined and united (in this case justice, which apportions happiness according to goodness of conduct).

come worthy of it through his good conduct. The justice of the judgment must be unexceptionable and unrelenting.

We meet with a symbol of this in the well-ordered government of a country. The only difference is that in such a government the powers of legislation, government, and justice are found in different persons, whereas in God they are all combined. In a state, the lawgiver must be sovereign, one whom nobody can evade. The administrator of the laws (who provides for and proportionally rewards those who have become worthy of his benevolence by following the laws), must be subordinate to the lawgiver, because he too must conduct himself in accordance with the same laws. And finally, the judge must be most just and must look closely to see whether the apportionment of rewards is really in accordance with desert. If we now separate every human representation from this symbol, the pure concept we obtain will be precisely the one which constitutes the moral perfections of God. This idea of a threefold divine function is fundamentally very ancient, and seems to lie at the foundation of nearly every religion. Thus the Indians thought of Brahma, Vishnu, and Shiva; the Persians of Ormuzd, Mithra, and Ahriman; the Egyptians of Osiris, Isis, and Horus; and the ancient Goths and Germans of Odin, Freya, and Thor. In each case these gods were thought as three powerful beings constituting one divinity; to the first belonged the legislation, to the second, the government, and to the third, the judgment of the world.

Reason leads us to God as a holy lawgiver. Our inclination for happiness wishes him to be a benevolent governor of the world. And our conscience represents him to our eyes as a just judge. Here we see the need and also the motive for thinking of God as holy, benevolent, and just. Happiness is a system of ends which are contingent, because they are only necessary on account of the differences between subjects. For everyone can participate in happiness only in the measure that he has made himself worthy of it. But morality is an absolutely necessary system of *all* ends, and it is just this agreement of an action with the idea of a system which is the ground of its morality. Hence an action is evil when the universality of the principle from which it is performed is contrary to reason. Moral theology convinces us of God's existence with far more certainty than physicotheology. For the latter teaches us only that we have need of the existence of God as a hypothesis for the explanation of contingent appearances. This has been sufficiently shown in that part of cosmology which deals with contingent purposes. But morality leads us to the principle of *necessary* purposes, without which it would itself be only a chimaera.

Holiness is the absolute or unlimited moral perfection of the will. A holy being must not be affected with the least inclination contrary to morality. It must be *impossible* for it to will something which is contrary to moral laws. So understood, no being but God is holy. For every creature always has some needs, and if it wills to satisfy them, it also has inclinations which do not always agree with morality. Thus man can never be *holy* though of course he can be *virtuous*. For virtue consists precisely in *self-overcoming*. Someone is also called holy if he abhors something as soon as he knows it to be morally evil. But this concept of holiness is not sufficiently dignified for the thing itself which it is supposed to signify. It would be better never to call any creature perfectly holy, however perfect it may be; or at least not to understand it to be holy as God is holy. For he is like the moral law itself, thought of as personified.

Benevolence is an immediate well-pleasedness with the welfare of others. Pure and complete benevolence is to be found nowhere but in God. For every creature has needs which limit its inclination to make others happy; or at least these needs limit its ability to make such use of these inclinations that it may have no regard at all for its own welfare. But God is independent benevolence. He is not limited by any subjective ground, because he himself has no needs. To be sure, the application of his benevolence is limited *in concreto* by the constitution of the subject in which it is to be demonstrated. God's benevolence is something positive, but his *justice* is fundamentally only a negative perfection, because it limits his benevolence in the measure that we have not made ourselves worthy of it. God's justice therefore consists in the combination of benevolence with holiness. In other words, one could also call it a *true benevolence*.

[The Problem of Evil]

Against the moral perfection of God, reason raises many objections which are strong enough to lead many men astray and plunge them into despair. And it is just on this account that these perfections have been made the object of extensive philosophical investigations. Leibniz, among others, has attempted in his *Theodicy* to weaken these objections, or rather to finish them off entirely. Let us now look carefully at these objections ourselves and test our powers on them.

(1) The first objection is against God's *holiness*. If God is holy and hates evil, then whence comes this *evil*, which is an object of abhorrence to all rational beings and the ground of all intellectual abhorrence?

(2) The second objection is against God's benevolence. If God is benevolent and wills that men be happy, then whence comes all the *ill*[3] in the world, which is an object of abhorrence to everyone who meets with it and constitutes the ground of physical abhorrence?

(3) The third objection is against God's justice. If God is just, then whence comes the unequal apportionment of good and evil in the world, standing in no community with morality?

Now let us consider the first objection. Where does the evil in the world come from if the sole original source of everything is holy? This objection gains its strength primarily through the consideration that nothing can arise without its first predisposition having been made by its creator. What, then? Has a holy God himself placed a predisposition to evil in man's nature? Because they were unable to make sense of this, it occurred to men long ago to assume a special evil original being, who had wrested a part of all things from the holy original source and impressed its own essence on that part. But this manichaeism conflicts with human reason, since reason leads us to one single being of all beings, and it can only think of this being as supremely holy. What, then? Shall we derive evil from a holy God?

3. Evil = *Böse*. Ill = *Übel*.

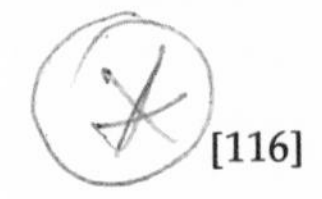

The following considerations will settle the matter for us. First, we must note that of all the many creatures there are, man is the only one who has to work for his perfections and for the goodness of his character, producing them from within himself. God therefore gave him talents and capabilities, but left it up to man himself how he would employ them. He created man free, but gave him also animal instincts; he gave man senses to be moderated and overcome through the development of his understanding. Thus created, man was certainly perfect both in his nature and as regards his predispositions. But regarding the development of these predispositions, he was still crude and uncultivated.[4] Man himself had to be responsible for this development, through the cultivation of his talents and the goodness of his will. Endowed with great capabilities, but with the application of these capabilities left to himself, such a creature must certainly be of significance. Much can be expected of him, but on the other hand, no less is to be feared. He can perhaps raise himself above a whole host of will-less angels,[5] but he may also degrade himself so that he sinks even beneath the irrational animals. To begin his cultivation he must step forth out of his uncultivated state, and free himself from his instincts. But what then will be his lot? Only false steps and foolishness. Yet who but man himself is responsible for them?

This way of representing the matter is in full agreement with the story of Moses, which describes the very same thing after a sensuous manner. In paradise man appears as nature's darling, great in his predispositions but crude in their cultivation. Thus he lives on undisturbed, led by his instincts, until finally he feels his humanity, and in order to prove his freedom, he *falls*. Now he no longer *is* an animal, but he has *become* an animal. He proceeds to develop himself, but with each new step he takes come

4. Crude and uncultivated = *roh*.

5. Kant is again alluding to Albrecht von Haller: *Denn Gott liebt keinen Zwang, die Welt mit ihren Mängeln / Ist besser als ein Reich von Willen-losen Engeln*. ("For God loves not compulsion; the world with all its faults / Is better than a realm of will-less angels.") Kant quotes these lines from Haller's poem *Über den Ursprung des Übels* (On the Origin of Evil) (1734) (Bk. ii, ll. 33–34) in the *Religion* (*Gesammelte Schriften*, vol. 6, p. 65n; cf. *Religion Within the Limits of Reason Alone* [New York, 1960], p. 58n.)

new false steps, and in this way he approaches ever nearer to the idea of perfection in a rational being. Yet he will perhaps not attain this idea for millions of years.

In this earthly world, there is only progress. Hence in this world goodness and happiness are not things to be possessed, they are only paths toward perfection and contentment. Thus the evil in the world can be regarded as the incompleteness in the development of the seed toward good. Evil has no special seed. For it is only a negation, and consists only in a limitation of what is good. It is nothing but the incomplete development of the seed of goodness out of its uncultivated condition. But the good does have a seed; for it is independent. The predisposition to good, which God has placed in man, must be developed by man himself before the good can make its appearance. But since at the same time man has many instincts belonging to animality, and since he has to have them if he is to continue being human, the strength of his instincts will beguile him, and he will abandon himself to them. It is from this that *evil* arises; or rather, he falls into *foolishness* as soon as he begins to use his reason. A special seed for evil is unthinkable.[6] It is rather the first development of our reason towards goodness which is the origin of evil. Or again, it is the uncultivatedness still remaining in the progress of man's cultivation which is evil. Evil, therefore, is inevitable. Does God, then, really will what is evil?

6. This discussion of evil antedates by some years Kant's discussion of the radical evil in human nature in the *Religion*. Here in the Lectures he attributes the origin of evil to Man's "uncultivatedness" (*Rohheit*), the incompleteness of man's moral development in disciplining his inclinations. The theory is very similar to that adopted by Hegel (cf. *Werke*, Frankfurt, 1970, p. 69; Hegel's *Philosophy of Right*, tr. T. M. Knox, Oxford, 1967, §18, pp. 28, 231). But such an account leaves unanswered the question: Why is this moral development necessary at all? In his writings prior to the *Religion*, Kant was at times disposed to regard this resistance to reason as a necessary property of inclinations, and of the finitude of man as a being of needs, from which they arise. But to do this, as he realized in the *Religion*, would be to treat one of man's "predispositions for good" (his "animality") as the ground of evil in his nature. Consequently, in the *Religion* Kant revises his view and attributes evil to an "original propensity" in man's own power of free choice (*Willkür*) to invert the moral order of incentives and make the satisfaction of his subjective desires the condition for fulfilling his duty. This doctrine shocked some of Kant's contemporaries (Goethe for instance) but in fact it is a much more thoughtful treatment of the problem than the one found in this passage.

By no means. For God wills that evil be eliminated, through the all-powerful development of the seed of perfection. He wills that evil be removed by the progress toward goodness. But evil is not a *means* to goodness. Rather it arises as a by-product, since man has to struggle with his own limits, his animal instincts. The means toward goodness lies in *reason*. This means is man's striving to pull himself out of his uncultivated condition. When man begins this striving, he first uses his reason to serve his instincts. But finally he develops it for its own sake. Thus evil is found only when man's reason has developed far enough for him to know his obligations. St. Paul himself says that sin follows upon the law.[7] If man finally developed himself completely, then evil would cease of itself. As soon as man knows his obligation to the good and yet does evil in spite of it, he becomes worthy of punishment, because he could have overcome his instincts. And even his instincts are placed in him for good; and when man pursues them to excess, it is he who is at fault and not God.

This *justifies* God's holiness, because by following this path the whole species of the human race will finally attain to perfection. But if we ask where the evil in individual men comes from, the answer is that it exists on account of the limits necessary to every creature. It is just as if we were to ask: Where do the parts of the whole come from?

But the human race is a class of creatures which through their own nature are some day to be released and set free from their instincts. During their development, many false steps and vices will arise. But the whole is some day to win through to a glorious outcome, though perhaps only after enduring many punishments for their weakness.. If I went so far as to ask why God created me, or mankind in general, this would certainly be presumptuousness, for it would be as much as to ask why God completed and joined together the great chain of natural things through the existence of a creature like man. Why did he not instead leave a gap? Or why didn't God make man an angel instead? But then would he have been man?

7. Romans 7:7.

There is another objection: If God has the actions of man in general in his power and guides them according to general laws, then he must also be the author of evil actions. But this is a transcendental objection and hence does not belong here. Rather it belongs to rational psychology, which deals with human freedom. Later on in our theory of providence we will show how we are to understand the claim that God concurs with the free actions of men.

The second objection, taken from the ill in the world, goes against God's *benevolence*. Hence now we want to investigate where the ill in the world comes from. We do have an idea of the complete whole of well-being and contentment. But we cannot cite a case *in concreto* where this idea of happiness is completely realized. There are two kinds of happiness:

(1) One consists in the *satisfaction of desires*. But desires always presuppose needs, which are why we desire something. Hence they presuppose sorrow and ill too. (2) But there is also the possibility of a kind of happiness which is *mere enjoyment*, without any needs. Any man who wanted to be happy in this way would be the most useless man in the world. For he would completely lack any incentives to action, since incentives consist in desires. Fundamentally we cannot even frame a correct concept of happiness for ourselves except by thinking of it as a *progress toward contentment*. This is why we are uneasy about the life-style of people who do almost nothing but eat, drink, and sleep. It would never occur to any man who is aware of the powers and impulses in himself toward activity to exchange his state for this supposed happiness, even if he had to struggle with all sorts of discomforts. Hence a novelist always permits his hero to withdraw from the stage once he has overcome his many difficulties and has finally achieved tranquillity. For the novelist is quite conscious of the fact that he cannot describe happiness as mere enjoyment. Rather, it is labor, difficulty, effort, the prospect of tranquillity, and the striving toward the achievement of this idea which is happiness for us, and a proof already of God's benevolence. The measure of happiness for a creature cannot be determined from one point in its existence. Rather God's aim is the happiness of creatures throughout the whole duration of their

existence. *Ill* is only a special arrangement for leading man toward happiness. Then again, we know too little of the outcome of suffering, of God's purposes in it, of the constitution of our nature and of happiness itself, to be able to determine the measure of happiness of which man is capable in this world. It is enough that it is within our power to render most ill harmless to us, indeed to make our world into a paradise, and to make ourselves worthy of an uninterrupted happiness. But ill is necessary if man is to have a wish and an aspiration toward a better state, and at the same time to learn how to strive to become worthy of it. If man must someday die, he must not only have sweetness here. Rather, the sum, the whole *facit* of his sufferings and his joys must finally be brought into relation. Is it possible to think of a better plan for man's destiny?

The third objection is against God's *justice*, and has this question as its object: Why in this world is there no proportion between good conduct and well-being? If we investigate this precisely, we find that the disproportion between the two is not really so large, and in the end *honesty* is the best attitude. We must not be blinded by the outward glitter that frequently surrounds the vicious man. If we look within him we always read, as Shaftesbury says, the admission of his reason: "Thou art nevertheless a villain."[8] The restlessness of his conscience torments him constantly, agonizing reproaches torture him continually, and all his apparent good fortune is really only self-decep-

8. This is not an exact quote. The passage Kant has in mind is probably the following: "There scarcely is, or can be any Creature, whom Consciousness of Villainy, as such merely, does not at all offend; nor anything opprobrious or heinously imputable, move, or affect. If there be such a one; 'tis evident he must be absolutely indifferent towards moral Good or Ill. If this indeed be his Case; 'twill be allow'd he can be no-way capable of natural Affection: If not of that, then neither of any social Pleasure, or mental Enjoyment, as shewn above; but on the contrary, he must be subject to all manner of horrid unnatural and ill Affection. So that to want CONSCIENCE, or *natural Sense of the Odiousness of Crime and Injustice*, is to be most miserable of all in Life; but where Conscience, or Sense of this sort, remains; there, consequently, whatever is committed against it, must of necessity, by means of Reflection, as we have shewn, be continually shameful, grievous and offensive" (Anthony Ashley Cooper, Third Earl of Shaftesbury, *Characteristicks of Men, Manners, Times*, Vol. II, Treatise IV: An Inquiry Concerning Virtue, or Merit [London, 1699], Bk. 2, Pt. 2, par. 1, pp. 121–122).

tion and disappointment. Nevertheless, we cannot deny that at times even the most righteous man would seem to be a ball in the hands of fate, as regards the external circumstances of fortune. But all morality, that is, all good conduct which is done merely because our reason commands it, would come to nothing if our true worth were determined by the course of things and the fate we meet with in it. Moral conduct would be transformed into a rule of *prudence*. Self-interest would be the incentive for our virtues. But to sacrifice one's peace, one's powers, and one's advantage when the external laws of morality demand it—only that is true virtue, and worthy of future recompense. If there were no disproportion at all between morality and well-being here in this world, there would be no opportunity for us to be truly virtuous.

Second Section: The Nature and Certainty of Moral Faith

Probability has a place only regarding the knowledge of things in the world. For anything of which I am to have probable knowledge must be homogeneous with (or a thing of the same kind as) some other thing of which my knowledge is certain. For instance, I know with probability that the moon is inhabited, because many similarities between it and the earth have been discovered (mountains, valleys, seas, and perhaps also an atmosphere). But this knowledge of the moon's habitability is probable only because I see with certainty that the earth is homogeneous with it in many ways, and from this I conclude that it would also be similar to it in this way. But when it is a question of a thing which does not belong to this world at all, then no homogeneity and hence no probability can apply to it. So I cannot say that it is probable that God exists. Such an expression would also be unsuited to the dignity of this knowledge. And it is improper too, because no analogy between God and the world is thinkable. Hence in this case I must be content to have knowledge of something, or at least to be fully convinced of its existence.

Conviction is of two kinds, *dogmatic* and *practical*. The former has to be sought in mere concepts a priori, and has to be apodictic. But we have already seen that by the path of mere speculation we cannot convince ourselves with certainty of God's existence. At most the speculative interest of our reason compels us to assume such a being as a subjectively necessary hypothesis. But reason has no capacity sufficient to *demonstrate* it. Our need makes us wish for such a demonstration, but our reason cannot lay hold of it. It is true that I can argue from the existence of the world and from its accidental appearances to the existence of some supreme original being. Yet there still remains to us another kind of conviction, a *practical* one. It is a special field, which gives us far more satisfying prospects than dry speculation can ever yield. For if something presupposed on subjective grounds is only a hypothesis, a presupposition on objective grounds is a necessary *postulate*. These objective grounds are either theoretical (as in mathematics) or practical (as in morality). For moral imperatives, since they are grounded in the nature of our being as free and rational creatures, have as much evidence and certainty as mathematical propositions originating in the nature of things ever could have. Thus a necessary practical postulate is the same thing in regard to our practical interest as an axiom is in regard to our speculative interest. For the practical interest which we have in the existence of God as a wise ruler of the world is as great as it possibly can be, since if we cancel this fundamental principle, we renounce at the same time all prudence and honesty, and we have to act against our own reason and our conscience.

[The *Absurdum Practicum*]

Such a moral theology not only provides us with a convincing certainty of God's being, but it also has the great advantage that it leads us to *religion*, since it joins the thought of God firmly to our morality, and in this way it even makes better men of us. Our moral faith is a practical postulate, in that anyone who denies it is brought *ad absurdum practicum*. An *absurdum logicum* is an absurdity in judgments; but there is an *absurdum practicum* when it is shown that anyone who denies this or that would have to be a scoundrel. And this is the case with moral faith. This moral belief is not one of my opinions concerning some hypothesis, that is, concerning some presupposition founded on contingent appearances. If one argues from the contingency of the world to a supreme author, then this is only a hypothesis, even if it is one which is necessary for us as an explanation, and hence something like a highly probable opinion. But such presuppositions, which flow from some absolutely necessary datum (as in morality and mathematics), are not mere opinions, but demand of us a firm belief. Hence our faith is not scientific knowledge, and thank heaven it is not! For God's wisdom is apparent in the very fact that we do not *know* that God exists, but should *believe* that God exists. For suppose we could attain to scientific knowledge of God's existence, through our experience or in some other way (even if the possibility of this knowledge cannot immediately be thought). And suppose further that we could really reach as much certainty through this knowledge as we do in intuition. Then in this case, all our morality would break down. In his every action, man would represent God to himself as a rewarder or avenger. This image would force itself involuntarily on his soul, and his hope for reward and fear of punishment would take the place of moral motives. Man would be virtuous out of sensuous impulses.

questionable

[God's Justice]

Baumgarten speaks of God's *sincerity*,[9] but this expression is far beneath the dignity of the highest being. For negative perfections like sincerity (which consists only in God's not behaving hypocritically) could only be predicated of God insofar as it might occur to someone to *deny* them. But sincerity and truth are already contained in the concept of God in such a way that anyone who rejected these attributes would have to deny God himself as well. Such perfections, moreover, are already contained in God's holiness, since a holy being would certainly

9. "SINCERITY is benevolence concerning what is signified in one's mind, and this is in God" (Baumgarten, *Metaphysica*, §919).

never lie. And why set up a special rubric and classification for each of the *corollaria*? If we really want to cite sincerity and truth as special attributes of God, it would be better to define them in terms of the sincerity and truth which God demands of us. So there are still only three moral attributes of God, the three we have treated above: holiness, benevolence, and justice.

We can think of God's justice in two ways: either as justice within the order of nature, or justice by special decree. But as long as we have no instruction concerning the latter, or as long as we can make everything given in nature harmonize with God's holiness and benevolence, it is our duty to stop with a justice which gives us what our deeds are worth in the present course of things. This justice within the order of nature consists in the fact that God has already laid down in the course of things, and in his universal plan for the world, the way in which man's state will be proportioned to the degree of morality he has attained. Well-being is inseparably combined with good conduct, just as punishment is combined with moral corruption. Moral perfection in this life will be followed by moral growth in the next, just as moral deterioration in this life will bring a still greater decline. After death man will continue with his development and the predisposition of his abilities. Thus if in this world he strives to act in a morally good way and gradually attains to moral accomplishment, he may hope to continue his moral improvement in the world to come. On the other hand, if he has acted contrary to the eternal and necessary laws of morality, and has gradually made himself worse by frequent transgressions, then he must fear that his moral corruption will continue and increase. Or at least he has no reason to believe that a sudden reversal will occur in the next life. Instead, the experience of his state in the world and in the order of nature in general gives him clear proof that his moral deterioration (and with it the essentially necessary punishment) will last indefinitely or eternally, just like moral perfection and the well-being inseparable from it.

God's justice is usually divided into (1) *justitiam remunerativam* and (2) *justitiam punitivam*, since God punishes evil and rewards

goodness.[10] But the rewards which God bestows on us proceed not from his justice, but from his benevolence. For if they came to us from justice, then there could be no *praemia gratuita* [gifts of grace]. We would have to possess some right to demand them, and God would have to be bound to give them to us. Justice gives nothing gratuitously, it gives to each only the reward he merits. But even if we unceasingly observe all moral laws, we can never do more than our duty. Hence we can never expect rewards from God's justice. Men may certainly merit things of one another and demand rewards based on their mutual justice. But we can give nothing to God, and so we can never have any right for rewards against him. It is written in a sublime and moving text: "He that hath pity on the poor lendeth to the Lord."[11] Here the reward which is due us for the sake of the unfortunate is ascribed to God's benevolence, and God himself is regarded as our debtor. It is represented that when God bestows a promise on us, we are justified in demanding what he has promised us and expecting from his justice that it will be fulfilled. But promises of this kind, where someone pledges a wholly undeserved benefit to another, do not appear actually to bind the promisor to grant this benefit to the other. Or at least they do not give him the right to demand it. For they always remain good deeds, bestowed on us undeservedly, and they carry the mark not of justice but of benevolence. Hence in God there is no *justitiam remunerativam* toward us.[12] Instead, all the rewards he shows us must be ascribed to his benevolence. His justice is concerned only with punishment. These punishments are either (1) *poenae correctivae* [punishments for correction], (2) *poenae exemplares* [punishments for an example], or (3) *poenae*

10. "A REWARD (remuneration) is some good contingent on the moral goodness of a person. Justice in conferring rewards is REMUNERATIVE JUSTICE (*Iustitia Remuneratoria*), which we venerate in God in the highest degree. . . . Justice in imposing punishment is PUNITIVE JUSTICE (*Iustitia Punitiva*) (vindictive, avenging, vindicating, nemesis); punitive justice belongs to God" (Baumgarten, *Metaphysica*, §§907, 910).

11. Proverbs 19:17.

12. Kant evidently takes Baumgarten to be saying that in bestowing rewards out of "remunerative justice" God would only be giving us something he *owed* us, rather than performing an act of benevolence.

vindicativae [vindictive punishments]. The first two are given *ne peccatur* [not on account of any wrongdoing]; the third, *quia peccatum est* [because there is wrongdoing]. But all *poenis correctivis* and *poenis exemplaribus* are always grounded on *poenae vindicativae*. For an innocent man may never be punished as an example for others unless he deserves the punishment himself. Hence all corrective punishments ordained for the guilty as a warning to others, must always accord with the rules of justice. Hence they must be avenging punishments. But the expression *poenae vindicativae,* like the expression *justitia ultrix* [avenging justice], is really too harsh.[13] For we cannot think of vengeance in God, because vengeance always presupposes a feeling of pain impelling one to do something similar to the offender. So it is better to regard the punishments inflicted by divine justice on sins in general as an actus of *justitiae distributivae* [distributive justice], that is, as a justice limiting the apportionment of benevolence by the laws of holiness. Hence we see that there must be *poenae vindicativae,* because they alone constitute what is proper to justice; if they were rejected, this attribute could not be assumed in God at all. For *poenae correctivae* and *exemplares* are really acts of benevolence, because they promote what is best either for the individual men improved by them or for the whole people for whom the punishment serves as a warning. How, then, is the essence of divine justice to be posited in them? His justice must limit benevolence so that it distributes good only according to the subject's worthiness. Hence justice will not ordain punishments for the criminal merely in order to teach what is best for him or for someone else. Rather, it does so in order to punish the offense by which he has violated the law and made himself unworthy of happiness. These retributive punishments will become obvious only when our whole existence is considered, and hence can be correctly determined and appraised only in it. It is from this that we get the majestic idea of a universal judgment of the world.

The *patience* of God consists in the fact that he executes his punishment of evil in the criminal only after he has given him

13. As we have seen, Baumgarten does use the expressions *vindicatiua* (vindictive) and *ultrix* (avenging) in his description of God's punitive justice.

the opportunity to improve himself.[14] But after that, God's justice is unrelenting. For a judge who *pardons* is quite unthinkable. A judge must rather weigh all conduct strictly according to the laws of holiness and allow to each only that measure of happiness which is proportionate to his worthiness. It is enough to expect from God's benevolence that in this life it gives us the capacity to observe the laws of morality and to become worthy of happiness. God himself, the all-benevolent, can make us worthy of his good deeds. But unless we become worthy of this through our morality, God the just still cannot make us participants in happiness.

Impartiality belongs to those attributes which should not be special predicates of God.[15] For no one could doubt that it belongs to him, because it is already contained in the concept of a holy God. God's impartiality consists in the fact that God has no favorites. For this would presuppose some predilection in him, and it is only a human imperfection (as, for example, when parents have a special love for a child which has not especially distinguished itself). But it cannot be thought of God that he would choose some individual subject over others as his favorite, with no regard to the subject's worthiness; for this would have to be an anthropomorphic representation. But if it should happen that one nation becomes enlightened sooner than another and is brought nearer to the destination of the human species, then this would belong rather to the wisest plan of a universal providence, which we are in no position to survey. It is far from a proof that God has a special interest in this nation and cares about this people with a particular favor. For in the kingdom of ends as in the kingdom of nature, God governs according to universal laws, which do not appear to be in conjunction with our shortsighted understanding. Man is certainly in the habit of taking any special bit of undeserved good fortune befalling him for a special testimony of the favor of divine provi-

14. "FORBEARANCE (the patience of a judge) is justice which does not look for occasions to punish. God infallibly knows all the opportunities for punishment and all the proximate matters for punishment where they are real; but he wills [punishments] proportionately. Hence he is the most forbearant" (Baumgarten, *Metaphysica*, §916).

15. Baumgarten speaks of God's *impartialitas* (*Metaphysica*, §917).

dence. But this is the work of our self-preference, which would gladly persuade us that we are really worthy of the happiness we enjoy.

Equity is also a property which is beneath the majesty of the supreme being.[16] For we can think of genuine equity only among human beings. Equity is an obligation arising from the right of another insofar as it is not combined with a license to compel someone else. Hence it is distinguished from strict right, where I can compel someone else to fulfill his obligation. For instance, if I have promised to give a servant a certain allowance, then I must pay it to him whatever happens. But now suppose there comes a time of scarcity, so that the servant cannot live on the agreed wages. In this case according to strict right I have no obligation to accord him more for his maintenance than I have promised him. He cannot compel me to do so, since he has no further obligation as a ground for his rights. But it is only equitable that I not let him go hungry, and that I add to his wages a proportion large enough that he can live on it. Before the bar of conscience it counts as a strict right that I owe to others what is due them merely from equity. And even if everyone were to think me just, because I fulfill everything to which I can be compelled and to which I have an external obligation, my conscience will still reproach me if I have offended the rules of equity. And God judges according to our conscience, which is his representative here on earth.

Absolute *immortality,* the impossibility of perishing, is ascribed to God.[17] This attribute belongs by right only and solely to him, as a consequence of the absolute necessity of his existence. But the expression *immortality* is improper, because it is only a mere negation of an anthropomorphic representation. It is to be remarked in general that in theory the concept of God must be carefully purified and freed of all such human ideas; from a practical point of view, though, we may momentarily

16. "Impartial justice is EQUITY. God is most just and most impartial, so he is most equitable" (Baumgarten, *Metaphysica,* §918).

17. "Since God's highest life is absolutely necessary (for it is his essence itself and his existence), God is not only immortal, but *only he has absolute immortality*" (Baumgarten, *Metaphysica,* §922).

represent God using such predicates whenever by this means the thought of God affords more power and strength to our morality. But in the present case it is much better to use the expression *eternal* rather than *immortal*, since it is nobler and more appropriate to the dignity of God.

[God's Blessedness]

Since Baumgarten praises God as the *most happy being*, it will be necessary for us to investigate the true concept of happiness to see whether it fits God.[18] Pleasure in one's state is called *welfare*. And insofar as this pleasure applies to the whole of our existence, it is called *happiness*. Happiness is consequently pleasure in our state as a whole. Pleasure in one's own person is called *self-contentment*. But freedom constitutes that that which is most proper to us. Consequently, self-contentment is a pleasure in one's own freedom, or in the quality of one's will. If this self-contentment were to extend to the whole of our existence, it would be called *blessedness*. The distinction between self-contentment and happiness is just as necessary as it is important. For one can be fortunate, and in that sense, happy, without being blessed, even though the consciousness of one's own worth or self-contentment belongs to a perfect happiness.[19] But self-contentment can certainly be found without good fortune, because at least in this life good conduct is not always combined with well-being. Self-contentment arises from morality, while happiness depends on physical conditions. No creature has the powers of nature in its control, so as to be able to make them agree with its self-contentment. Hence the highest degree of self-contentment (or in other words, blessedness) cannot be ascribed to any creature. But we can be more fortunate, and in that sense happier, if our whole state is such that we are able to be well-pleased with it. Yet in the present life happiness itself will hardly be our lot, and the stoics probably exaggerated

18. Translating the following passage is made more difficult by the fact that Kant uses the adjective *glücklich* to refer both to happiness (*Glückseligkeit*) and to good fortune (*Glück*). Hence *glücklich* has been translated both as "happy" and as "fortunate," depending on which reference seemed to be intended.

19. Fortunate, and in that sense happy = *glücklich*.

things considerably when they believed that in this world virtue is always coupled with being well-pleased. The most infallible witness against this is experience.

For man, good fortune is not a possession, but a progression towards happiness. Yet full self-contentment, the comforting consciousness of integrity, is a good which can never be stolen from us, whatever the quality of our external state may be. And in fact all earthly happiness is far outweighed by the thought that as morally good men we have made ourselves worthy of an uninterrupted future happiness. Of course, this inner pleasure in our own person can never compensate for the loss of an externally happy state. But it can still uplift us even in the most troubled life when it is combined with its future prospects.

Now let us raise the question whether happiness may be ascribed to God. Since happiness relates only to one's external state, we must first ask whether God can be thought of as in a state. And then we first have to see what a state is. The ontological definition of a state is this: the coexistence of the changeable determinations of a thing along with the constant ones. In man, for instance, the constant determination is that he is human, and the changeable determinations are whether he is learned or ignorant, rich or poor. This coexistence of his changeable determinations (such as wealth or poverty) with the constant one (his humanity) constitutes his state. But in God everything is permanent. For how could changeable determinations be thought in him, existing along with what is constant in his essence? And how then can the eternal be thought of as in a state? But if no state can be predicated of God, then a state of happiness cannot be ascribed to him either. But supreme blessedness, the greatest possible self-contentment, belongs to him of itself; a blessedness, in fact, so understood that no creature can ever boast of anything even similar to it. For with creatures many external, sensible objects have an influence on their inner pleasure. But God is completely independent of all physical conditions. He is conscious of himself as the source of all blessedness. He is as it were the moral law itself personified. Hence he is also the only blessed one.

At the conclusion of moral theology it should be remarked

that the three articles of moral faith, *God, freedom* of the human will, and a *moral world,* are the only articles in which it is permissible for us to transport ourselves in thought beyond all experience and out of the sensible world; only here may we assume and believe something from a practical point of view for which we otherwise have no adequate speculative grounds.[20] But however necessary and dependable this procedure may be for the purposes of our morality, we are in no way justified in admitting ourselves further into this idea, and venturing to go with our speculation to a region with which only our practical interest is concerned. If we do so, then we are *fanatics*. For at this point the limits of our reason are clearly indicated, and whoever dares to transcend them will be punished by reason itself for his boldness with both pain and error. But if we remain within these boundaries, then our reward will be to become wise and good men.

Third Section: The Causality of God

God's causality, or his *relation to the world*, can be considered in *three* respects: (1) In *nexu effectivo*, insofar as God is really the *cause* of the world and it is his *effectus*. (2) In *nexu finali*, insofar as God has willed the attainment of certain aims by his production of the world. Here God is considered as the *author* of the world, that is, as a cause of the world through intention. (3) In *nexu morali*. Here we come to know God as the *ruler* of the world.

I. God as Cause of the World

All the concepts in which men have ever thought of God as the world's cause can be brought under the following classification: (1) God has been represented as the world itself. This was called *pantheism* in ancient times, and *Spinozism* in modern. In general, it may be called the *systema inhaerentiae*. (2) Or, alterna-

20. More often, Kant describes the three postulates as God, freedom, and *immortality*. But in Reflexion 8101, Kant describes faith in immortality as "faith of the second rank" and suggests that it may not be necessary to the moral life after all (*Gesammelte Schriften*, vol. 19, p. 644).

tively, God has been thought of as an *ens extramundanum*. But then his causality has been conceived in either of two ways: (a) First, the attempt has been made to explain it from the necessity of his nature. This is the *systema emanationis*.[21] It is either *crassior*, as when one represents the substances of the world as arising through division (but this is absurd); or *subtilor*, where the origin of all substances is considered to be an emanation of God. (b) Or second, God's causality has been explained through his freedom. This is the *systema liberi arbitrii*, in which God is represented as the creator of the world.

The subtler system of emanation, which regards God as the cause of substances by the necessity of his nature, has opposed to it one ground of reason which at once overthrows it. This ground is taken from the nature of an absolutely necessary being and consists in the fact that the actions which an absolutely necessary being undertakes from the necessity of its nature can never be any but those internal actions which belong to the absolute necessity of its essence. For it is unthinkable that such a being should produce anything outside itself which is not also absolutely necessary. But how can something produced by something else be thought of as absolutely necessary? Yet if it is contingent, then how could it have emanated from a nature which is absolutely necessary? Every action performed by such a being from the necessity of its nature is immanent and can only concern its essence. Other things external to it can only be produced by it *per libertatem*. For otherwise, they are not things external to it, but belong to the absolute necessity of its own essence and are therefore internal to it.

This ground sets up a resistance on the part of reason toward the system of emanation, which regards God as cause of the world by the necessity of his nature. At the same time, it lays bare the cause of the unwillingness to accept this system which everyone feels, even if he is not always able to develop it clearly. It is an altogether different matter when we see one thing arise from another by the necessity of its nature within the world itself. For here cause and effect are homogeneous, as for instance

21. "CREATION BY EMANATION is the actualization of the universe from the essence of God" (Baumgarten, *Metaphysica*, §927).

in the generation of animals and plants. But it would be absurd to think of God as homogeneous with the totality of the world, because this would wholly contradict the concept of an *entis originarii*. For, as we have shown above, an *ens originarium* has to be isolated from the world. Hence there remains to our reason only the opposite system of causality, the *systema per libertatem*.

II. God as Author of the World[22]

[*Creation*.] As *autor mundi*, God can be thought of either: (1) Merely as the author of the forms of things; in this way we regard God only as the *architect* of the world; or (2) As the author of the very matter of substance in the world as well; and then God is the *creator* of the world.

In the world itself, only the forms of things arise and perish; substances themselves are permanent. An apple, for instance, arises because the tree forces fluids up through its stems and composes them. But the fluids themselves, where did the tree get them? From the air, the earth, the water, and so on. This matter is found in the apple too; but it exists in a different composition, a different form. Now here is another example, an example of perishing. When we remove the phlogiston from iron, its whole form is changed; it decomposes into dust and is no longer iron at all to ordinary eyes. But the substance of the iron remains undisturbed. For when new phlogiston is blown into it, the old form is restored and the iron dust becomes firm and solid. This form is contingent; the changes in it testify to this. Hence they must have an author, who gave them their initial arrangement. But the substances of the world are just as contingent as the forms, even if we do not perceive any changes in them. This is clear from their reciprocal *commercium*, the relationship in which they stand to each other as parts of a whole world. In ancient times it was always assumed that the matter of things, the fundamental material out of which all their forms arise, is eternal and necessary. Hence God was considered only as the world's *architect*, and matter was considered to be the

22. "An AUTHOR (*Avctor*) is a cause of free actions, and such actions as are caused by it and are the effects of an author are DEEDS (*Facta*). Now God is the author of creation and of this world" (Baumgarten, *Metaphysica*, §940).

building material out of which he formed all things. Fundamentally, then, only two principles were assumed by the ancients: God and Nature. This view served admirably to lay the blame for the greater part of the world's ills on the original properties of matter, without detracting from the wisdom and benevolence of the architect. Matter was held responsible because the eternal attributes of its nature were supposed to have placed many obstacles in the way of God's will when he tried to form it to his purposes. But this opinion was rejected as soon as philosophical ideas were further determined and refined; and rightly so. For it was seen that if matter occasions the ill in the world owning to its uselessness for certain aims, then it might also occasion much that is good through its fitness and agreement with other purposes. Hence it would be difficult to determine the extent to which God as the world's architect is responsible for what is good and bad in the world, and the extent to which matter, as its fundamental material, is responsible. But indeterminate ideas of this kind are useless in theology. Also, the contradiction was finally noted between saying that substances are eternal and necessary, and yet that they nevertheless have an *influxum mutuum* [mutual influence] on each other. The confusion and absurdity in the view that the whole world consists of many necessary things finally put human reason on the track of *creation from nothing*, a doctrine of which the ancients hardly had the least concept. Matter was now viewed as a product of God's free will, and God was thought of not only as the world's architect, but also as its creator. But for a long time the idea of an independent matter persisted in the heads of philosophers, and even of orthodox ones. Hence there were jealous outcries against anyone who ventured to explain part of the world's order and beauty from universal laws of nature. For some were concerned that in this way such arrangements would be snatched away from God's supreme rule. But this could be believed only by someone who thinks of matter as independent of God, like a coordinated principle. Yet if it is assumed that every substance receives its origin from God, then all matter is subordinated to God and all its laws in the last analysis have their origin in him. But creation out of nothing appears to contradict the metaphysical proposition: *ex nihilo nihil fit*. Yet this proposition can only be true for what is highest in the world itself. In this world it can be rightly said that no substance can arise which has not already been in existence at some previous time. And this is what the above proposition means to say. But when it is a question of the origin of the world as a whole, and the creation of the world is not thought of as something given in time (since time began only with it), then there is no difficulty in thinking that the whole universe might have arisen through the will of an extramundane being, even if nothing was previously in existence. But we must guard against mixing in the concepts of time, of arising, and of beginning at this point; for this would produce only confusion. We must even admit that such a production of substances (and hence the possibility of creation) is something which cannot be comprehended by human reason, since we are not in a position to cite any similar case *in concreto* where a substance arises before our eyes. In general there are many difficulties associated with the production of one substance by another. Is this production to be through emanation or freedom? And could there be any substance subsisting entirely for itself? These difficulties will probably always remain in part insoluble. But this is certainly not a sufficient ground for doubting the system of creation itself, since the subject matter here is of such a kind that we can probably never attain to a clear insight into it. It is enough that we feel the urge in some way to assume it as something given, and to have a firm belief in it. For speculative reason must always admit that this idea is the most rational of any, and the one most suited to reason's own use.

Creation, or actualization out of nothing, refers only to substances. The forms of these substances, different as they may be, arise from the particular modifications of their composition. Hence every substance produced out of nothing is a *creature*. But even if the substance itself as well as its form comes from God, we may still ask whether one substance can be thought as the *creatrix* of another. And to this the answer is: absolutely not. For all substances, as parts of the whole world, are in a reciprocal *commercio*, and have a mutual influence on each other. Thus each substance acts on the others and is passive to them as well. If this were not so, then all the substances together could not constitute a whole, with each substance as part of the whole. But if this is so, then it is unthinkable that one substance could be the author of another, since the second substance must act on the first as well as being passive to it. But in this case it is a *contradictio in adjecto* for one substance to be the author of another. Suppose for instance that someone built a house and then was killed when it collapsed. Now in this case he could be thought as the cause of what he suffered. But he made only the mere form of the house, by composing the building materials. He did not himself generate the substance, the matter. But it was just this matter, of which he was not the author or cause, which worked its influence on him and caused his death. Hence even God cannot be thought as having reciprocal influence on the world. He acts on everything but is passive to nothing. God's creation has to have been complete at once and instantaneously. For in God only one infinite act can be thought, a single, lasting power which created the whole world instantaneously and which maintains it in eternity. Through this power, many powers were poured out all at once into the world as a whole, and then they developed gradually in it according to universal laws.

As we have already remarked, creation applies merely to substances. Hence if it is said that the creation of the world happened all at once, it is only the creation of substances that is to be understood. These substances, therefore, always remain constant and their number neither increases nor decreases. God creates only once. Hence it cannot be asserted that even now God is creating a world, at least in the sense we mean here. No new substances ever arise, but many new forms can arise in the world, when the matter already present is composed in some different way. Fundamentally only one action can be thought in God, for in him there is no succession. But this one act may have, and actually does have, an infinite number of relations and expressions, according to the constitution of the subjects to which it refers. Hence at times God's power is not at all visible to us, while at other times we are far more sensible of it.

God acts no way but *freely*. Nothing has any influence on

him, so as to be able to move him to act in any particular way. For in an absolutely necessary being there are no determinations which might impel him to actions other than those he wills out of his greatest freedom. Thus he also created the world out of free will.

That the world created by God is the *best* of all possible worlds, is clear for the following reason.[23] If a better world than the one willed by God were possible, then a will better than the divine will would also have to be possible. For indisputably that will is better which chooses what is better. But if a better will is possible, then so is a being who could express this better will. And therefore this being would be more perfect and better than God. But this is a contradiction; for God is *omnitudo realitatis*. There is more on this subject in my essay on optimism.[24]

According to Leibniz, all the objections to this theory based on the existence of so much ill in the world can be immediately disproved as follows. Since our earth is only a part of the world, and since each part must be incomplete in itself (because only the whole totality of the world is supposed to be the best), it is impossible to determine whether ill would have to belong even to the best world as regards the plan for the whole. For if someone demanded that our earth be free of all ill, and hence wholly good, he would be acting just as if he wanted one part to be the whole.[25] Thanks be to the astronomers who, by their observations and inferences, have elevated our concept of the world as

23. "In creating this world, God decreed according to his most proportional will. Hence he decreed the existence of this world for the sake of the degree of good he recognized in it. . . . Therefore, this world is of all possible [worlds] the most perfect" (Baumgarten, *Metaphysica*, §§934–935). Kant, along with Baumgarten, accepts the Leibnizian doctrine that this is the best of all possible worlds. For Kant, however, this is a postulate of moral faith, not something demonstrable by speculative metaphysics.

24. Kant was a much more orthodox Leibnizian in his 1759 essay *Versuch einiger Betrachtungen über den Optimismus* (An Attempt at Some Considerations concerning Optimism), *Gesammelte Schriften*, vol. 2, pp. 27–36.

25. Cf. Leibniz, *On the Ultimate Origin of Things* (1697) (*Philosophischen Schriften*, vol. 7, pp. 303, *Leibniz: Selections*, ed. Philip Wiener, New York, 1951, pp. 351–352). The argument is stated most precisely in *Theodicy* (1710), §§213–215: "The part of the best whole is not necessarily the best which could have been made of that part. For the part of a beautiful thing is not always beautiful, since it can be extracted from the whole or taken in the whole in an irregular

a whole far above the small circle of our world. For they have not only provided us with a broader acquaintance with the whole, but they have also taught us modesty and caution in our judgments about it. For surely if our terrestrial globe were the whole world, it would be difficult to know it for the best, and to hold by this with conviction. For to speak honestly, on this earth the sum of sorrow and the sum of good might very well just about balance each other. Yet even in sorrow there are incentives to activity, and so one might even call it beneficial in itself. For instance the stinging flies in a swampy place are nature's call to men to drain the mires and make them arable, in order to get rid of these disagreeable guests. Or, if we did not feel the pain of a wound and were not thus impelled to concern ourselves with healing it, we might bleed to death from it.

But it is possible to know the doctrine of the best world from maxims of reason alone, independent of all theology and without it being necessary to resort to the wisdom of a creator in proof of it. This can be done in the following way: In the whole of organized nature it must be assumed as a necessary maxim of our reason that in every animal and plant there is not the least thing which is useless and without purpose; on the contrary, it must be assumed that everything contains a means best suited to certain ends. This is a principle taken for granted in the study of nature, and every experiment made has confirmed it. Setting these experiments aside, the field of discoveries would be closed to the anatomist. Hence the cultivation of our own reason urges us to assume and use this maxim. But if the whole of organized (yet irrational) nature is arranged in something like the best way, then we should expect things to be similar in the nobler

---

manner. If goodness and beauty always consisted in something absolute and uniform . . . it would be necessary to say that the part of what is good and beautiful would also be good and beautiful. But this is not so with things involving relations (*choses relatives*). . . . In some parts of the universe, we find defects which the author of things allowed because otherwise, if he had reformed the faulty part and made a satisfactory composite of it, the whole would not be as beautiful as it is. . . . [Hence] I answer that since God chooses the best possible, one cannot object to any limitation in his perfections. And not only does good surpass evil in the universe, but in fact the evil serves to augment the good" (Leibniz, *Philosophischen Schriften*, vol. 6, pp. 245–247).

part of the world, in rational nature. But the same law is valid also for organized creatures and for the mineral kingdom, for the sake of the necessary harmony in which everything is combined under the supremely necessary principle of unity. For reason's sake, therefore, we can and must assume that everything in the world is arranged for the best, and that the whole of everything existing is the best possible one.

This doctrine has the same influence on morality as it has on natural science. For if I cannot be sure that the laws governing the course of nature are the best ones, then I must also doubt whether in such a world true well-being will eventually be combined with my worthiness to be happy. But if this world *is* the best one, then my morality will stand firm and its incentives will retain their strength. For now I can be certain that in a best world it is impossible for good conduct to exist apart from well-being; and that even if for a certain part of my existence the course of things does not look this way, it would certainly have to hold for my existence as a whole if this world is to be the best one. Hence even our *practical* reason takes a great interest in this doctrine and knows it to be a necessary presupposition for its own sake and without founding it on theology. From the above discussion it is already clear how evil[26] could be found in a best world, as a by-product of the progress toward moral goodness.

The Purpose of Creation. It is possible to think of a double purpose of creation. First, an objective purpose, consisting in the perfection which made the world an object of God's will; and second, a subjective purpose. Yet what kind of incentive (if one may so express it) could move God to create a world? But the next section will deal with this latter purpose; the first purpose is the object of our present investigation.

Now what is the perfection for which God created the world? We may not seek such a purpose in irrational creatures. For everything in these creatures is only a means to higher purposes which can only be reached by the correct use of these means. The true perfection of the world as a whole has to lie in the use *rational* creatures make of their reason and freedom. It is only

26. Pölitz's text reads *Beste*. I assume Kant means *Böse*.

here that *absolute* ends can be proposed, since reason is always required for something intentional. But what is this right use which rational creatures are to make of the will? It is a use such as can stand under the principle of the system of all ends. A universal system of ends is only possible according to the idea of morality. Hence only the fulfillment of the moral law is a rightful use of our reason. So the perfection of the world will consist in the fact that it is congruent with morality; for it is morality alone which makes possible a system of all ends.

A system of all ends can be thought in two ways: either (1) through freedom or (2) in the nature of things. A system of ends through freedom can be attained by means of the principles of morality, and this is the moral perfection of the world. Rational creatures have value as persons only insofar as they can be regarded as members of this universal system. For a good will is something good in and for itself, and hence something *absolutely* good. Everything else is only a conditioned good. Sharpness of mind, for instance, or health, is good only under the right condition, that is when it is rightly used. But since morality makes possible a system of all ends, it gives to the rational creature a value in and for himself, by making him a member of this great kingdom of ends. The possibility of such a universal system of all ends depends solely on morality. For it is only insofar as all rational creatures act according to these eternal laws of reason that they can stand under a principle of community and together constitute a system of all ends. For example, if all men speak the truth, then a system of ends is possible among them; but if only one should lie, his end is no longer combined with the others. Hence the universal rule for judging the morality of an action is always this: If all men did this, could there still be a combination of ends?

The physical perfection of the world is the system of all ends in accordance with the nature of things; and it is attained along with the rational creature's worthiness to be happy. It is only in this way that the state of a creature may obtain a preeminent value. Without such a physical perfection of the world, the rational creature might certainly have an excellent value in himself, but his state could still be bad; and vice versa. But if both moral and physical perfection are combined, then we have the best world. Hence God's objective purpose in creation was the perfection of the world, and not merely the happiness of creatures; for this constitutes only physical perfection. A world with it alone would still be lacking in moral perfection, or the worthiness to be happy. Or is the perfect world to be one whose members overflow with pleasure and good fortune while nevertheless being conscious that their own existence itself is without value?

But apart from these *objective* grounds for being well-pleased with some matter and its constitution, there are also *subjective* grounds for pleasure in the existence of a thing. These two grounds have to be distinguished from each other. For I can find a thing to be very fine indeed on objective grounds, but still be indifferent to its existence as far as I myself am concerned. Here there is no subjective ground for my pleasure; or in a word, for my interest. This often holds in the case of moral motives.[27] For if these motives are objective, they certainly obligate me to do something, but they do not grant me the powers and incentives to do it. If I am to perform actions which I know to be right and good, I also require certain subjective motives to impel me actually to put these actions into practice. It is necessary for this not only that I judge the deed to be fine and noble, but my choice must also be determined by this judgment as well. But now it will be asked: In creating the world, did God have a subjective incentive determining his choice in addition to the objective ground of its perfection? And if he did have one, what was it? But in God no incentive is thinkable except an objective motive. His causality is determined only by the idea of a perfect object, combined with the consciousness of himself as a sufficient ground of every perfection.

For if before God actualized anything some further subjective pleasure in the existence of this thing had to be added as an incentive to his causality, then a part of his blessedness would have to depend on the existence of the thing in which he takes this interest. For his pleasure in the perfection of the thing in its

27. Ground = *Grund*. Motive = *Bewegungsgrund*.

idea alone would not be strong enough to move him to produce it; and God would have need of a special interest in the actual existence of the thing. Consequently, God would have need of the existence of a world in order to enjoy a complete blessedness. But this would contradict his highest perfection.

Hence we have to make a distinction between a *voluntas originaria* [original will] and a *voluntas derivativa* [derivative will]. It is only the latter which has need of special incentives to determine it to the choice of something good. For instance, on objective grounds a man can find a deed thoroughly noble, but he may nevertheless hesitate to perform it because he believes he has no particular subjective motives for doing so. A completely perfect will, on the other hand, would do the deed merely because it is *good*. The perfection of the thing it wills to produce is by itself a sufficient motive for it actually to put the deed into practice. Hence God created a world because he was most well-pleased with its highest perfection, where every rational creature would participate in happiness to the measure in which he had become worthy of it. In short, he created a world for the sake of its physical as well as its moral perfection. Thus one must not say that God's motive in creating the world was only the happiness of his creatures, as if God could take pleasure in seeing other beings happy without their being worthy of it. On the contrary, God's infinite understanding knew the possibility of a *highest good* external to himself, in which morality would be the supreme principle. And he was also conscious of having all the power needed to set up this most perfect of all possible worlds. His well-pleasedness in this consciousness of himself as an all-sufficient ground was therefore the only thing determining his will to actualize the highest finite good. Hence it would be better to say that God created the world for his honor's sake because it is only through the obedience to his holy laws that God can be honored.[28] For what does it mean to honor God? What, if not to serve him? But how can he be served? Certainly not by

28. Baumgarten holds that God created the world for the sake of his own honor, or to be more precise, for the sake of his glory. But this claim has a meaning for him very different from the one it has for Kant. For Baumgarten, it is only a version of the rationalist doctrine (repudiated by Kant, as we have seen) that

trying to entice his favor by rendering him all sorts of praise. For such praise is at best only a means for preparing ourselves, and elevating our own hearts to a good disposition. Instead, the service of God consists simply and solely in following his will and observing his holy laws and commands. Thus morality and religion stand in the closest connection with one another. They are distinguished from one another only by the fact that in the former moral duties are carried out from the principle belonging to every rational being, which is to act as a member of a universal system of ends; whereas in the latter these duties are regarded as commandments of a supremely holy will, because fundamentally the laws of morality are the only ones which agree with the idea of a highest perfection.

The whole world can be regarded as a universal system of all ends, whether through nature or through freedom. This theory of ends is called teleology. But just as there is a physical system of ends, in which every thing in nature has a reference as a means to some end found in rational creatures, so there is also a practical system of ends, that is, a system in accordance with the laws of free volition. In this system, every rational creature is combined with every other as reciprocal end and means. The former system of ends is the object of *theologia physica* [natural theology]; the latter is treated by *theologia practica seu pneumatica* [practical or spiritual theology]. In it all rational creatures are themselves regarded as possible means for the attainment of the

---

one's own perfection is the a priori end and motive of all rational activity. "HONOR is the recognition of a higher perfection in something. Greater honor is GLORY. God's glory therefore is the greater cognition of his own highest perfection" (Baumgarten, *Metaphysica*, §942). Earlier, however, Kant denied that God aimed at his own glory in creating the world. At the same time, he apparently agreed with Baumgarten when he asserted that God's reason (*Grund*) for producing the best world was his understanding of his own capacity to produce the best (i.e. his own highest perfection). But there is no contradiction here, since for Kant (though not for Baumgarten and the rationalists) the motive or ground of an action is not necessarily (and never *should* be) the same as its end or purpose. Hence God's *motive* for producing the best world is his own highest perfection. But his end is the best world itself, whose supreme goodness, as Kant here claims, consists in the honor rational beings give God by obeying his moral laws. In this way, Kant fits the divine will into the theory of volition which, in its earlier statements here in the Lectures, appeared to be much more suitable to finite human volition than to the will of God.

ends of rational creatures. In this way, the world may be displayed not merely *in nexu effectivo* as a combination of causes and effects like a machine, but also *in nexu finali* as a system of all ends. In *theologia practica* we see that rational creatures constitute the center of creation, and everything in the world has some reference to them. But they also have a reference to one another as mutual means. Yet we should not be led astray by the fact that history describes human conduct as if it were without order or purpose. Rather, we should believe nevertheless that despite the misuse of its freedom the human species is founded on a universal plan, and in accordance with this plan it will in the end attain to its highest possible perfection. For up to now we have surveyed the plan only in its individual parts and fragments.

To conclude our consideration of God as creator of the world, we must try to solve the cosmological problem as to whether he created the world within time or from eternity. Now would it not be an internal contradiction to say that God created the world from eternity? For then the world would have to be eternal, like God; and yet it is also supposed to be dependent on him. Yet if eternity here means the same as infinite time, then I become guilty of a *regressus in infinitum* and fall into an absurdity. But then can we think of the creation of the world only as within time? No, not this either. For when I say that the world had a beginning, I am thereby asserting that there was a time before the origin of the world; because every beginning of something is the end of a time just past, and the first moment of a subsequent time. But if there was a time before the world existed, then it must have been an empty time. And this is once again an absurdity. And God himself must have been *in* this time.

Now how can reason emerge from this conflict between its ideas?[29] What is the cause of this dialectical illusion? It lies in the fact that I am regarding time, a mere form of sensibility, a mere formal condition, and a phenomenon, as a determination of the *mundi noumenon*. All appearances, to be sure, are given only within time. But when I try to bring under the rule of time even the actuation of the substances themselves which are the rule of

29. The conflict Kant has just set up will be familiar to readers of the *Critique of Pure Reason* as the temporal half of the First Antinomy.

time even the actuation of the substances themselves which are the substratum of all appearances (and consequently also of my sensible representations), then I commit an obvious error, a *metabasis eis allo genos*. For I confuse things which do not belong together at all. At this point my reason comes to know its inability to raise itself above experience. For although it is in a position to show that all the objections of its opponents are fruitless and vain, it is still too weak to settle anything itself with apodictic certainty.

Providence. The actuation of the world's beginning is *creation*. The actuation of its duration is *conservation*.[30] Both apply only to substances. For of the accidents which adhere to these substances, it can be said neither that they were created nor that they are conserved. It would also be well to make a distinction between the concept of God as the world's architect and the concept of him as its creator. This distinction is just as important as the one between accident and substance. For in God only one act can really be thought. And this act never ceases, but expresses itself without variation or interruption. For no succession of states is to be found in God, and consequently no time. So how could his power operate only for a certain time, and then cease or be interrupted? Hence the same divine power which actuated the beginning of the world constantly actuates its duration. The same power required for the creation of substances is also needed for their conservation. Yet if every substance in the world can only have duration through a continuous *actus divinum*, it would appear that this deprives it of its very substance. But here it is fundamentally only an expression (*self-subsistence*) which causes the difficulty and the apparent contradiction. Of course we cannot substitute a more suitable expression for it because language does not have one; but we can prevent it from being misinterpreted by explaining it. A substance, a thing subsisting for itself, is a *quod non indiget subjecto inhaerentiae* [thing which needs no subject in which to inhere], that is, it exists without being the predicate of anything else. For instance, I am a substance, because I refer everything I do to

30. "The actuation of duration is CONSERVATION (*Conservatio*)" (Baumgarten, *Metaphysica*, §950).

myself, without needing something else to which to ascribe my actions as something inhering in it.

But I myself may nevertheless always have need of some other being for my own existence. And this being may be the author of my existence and duration without its having to be the author of my actions at the same time. Hence substance and accident must be carefully distinguished from cause and effect. For the two relations are wholly different. A thing can be a *causatum alterius* [thing caused by something else] (or have need of the existence of something else for its own existence) and still subsist for itself. But subsisting and existing *originarie* have to be distinguished from one another; for subsistence would involve a contradiction if something existing *originarie* also had to exist as a *causatum alterius*. This would be a false definition of substance, like the one sketched out by the well-meaning Spinoza; for through too great a dependence on Cartesian principles he understood a substance to be a thing *quod non indiget existentia alterius* [which needs something else in order to exist]. The result of all this is that it is incomprehensible how substances should have duration through the power of God; but it is not contradictory.

The causality of more than one cause is called a *concursus*. That is, several causes can be united to produce an effect. When this happens, several *concausae* [cooperating causes] concur. In such a case none of these cooperating causes is in itself sufficient to produce the effect. For otherwise its unification with another cause would not be necessary to give it a *complementum ad sufficientiam* [addition to the point of sufficiency]. But where there is a *causa solitaria* or solitary cause, there can be no *concursus*. In the first place, several causes are required for a *concursus*. But these causes also have to be *concausae*; that is, they must be coordinated with each other, and not subordinated one to the other. For if the causes are subordinated one to another, and constitute a chain or series of causes in which each is a particular link, then each link in the chain is the complete cause of the next, even if all together they have a common ground in the first cause. But then each considered in itself is still a *causa solitaria* and there is no *concursus*. If a *concursus* is to take place, then the causes have to be united and coordinated with one another; and one cause must make up for what the other fails to produce. Thus the effect is produced only by the causes being unified and working in community with each other.

Applying this to God, it is clear first of all that he does not concur in the existence of substances.[31] For substances contribute nothing to their own duration, and therefore they cannot themselves operate in union with God as *concausae* of their own conservation. In this case, there is only a subordination of causes, so that every substance has its ground in God as the *prima causa*, since the matter of every substance itself is created by him. But just for this reason, there can be no *concursus*. For if there were, the substance would have to be coordinated with God.

In the same way, there is no *concursus* of God in natural events. For just because they are events given in nature, it is presupposed already that their first proximate cause is in nature itself. Hence this cause must be sufficient to effect the event, even if the cause itself (like every natural cause) is grounded in God as the supreme cause.

Yet a *concursus* between God and events given in the world is still not impossible. For it is always thinkable that a natural cause is not by itself sufficient to produce a certain effect. In such a case, God might give it a *complementum ad sufficientiam;* but whenever he did this, it would *eo ipso* be a *miracle*. For we call it a miracle when the cause of a given event is *supernatural,* as it would be if God himself operated as *concausa* in the production of such a miracle. Hence if one ascribes to God a special dispensation and direction regarding events given in the world, then one is only predicating so many miracles of him.

But how about free actions? Can a *concursus divinus* be affirmed of them? Now in general speculative reason cannot comprehend the freedom of creatures, nor can experience prove it.

31. Baumgarten does hold that "God concurs mediately as efficient cause in all the actions of finite substances," and "concurs immediately as efficient cause, . . . actuating and conserving [them]" (*Metaphysica*, §954). It is this doctrine of a "GENERAL PHYSICAL CO-OPERATION OF GOD (*Concvrsvs Dei Physicvs Generalis*)" (*Metaphysica*, §958), which Kant rejects here and in the following paragraph.

But our practical interest requires us to presuppose that we can act according to the idea of freedom. Yet even if it is true that our will can decide something independently of every natural cause, it is still not in the least conceivable how God might concur in our actions despite this freedom, or how he could concur as a cooperating cause of our will.[32] For then *eo ipso* we would not be the author of our own actions, or at least not wholly so. Of course this idea of freedom is one which belongs to the intelligible world, and we know nothing of it beyond the fact that it exists. So we do not know the laws by which it is governed. But even if our reason cannot deny the possibility of this *concursus*, it still sees that such an effect would have to be a miracle of the *moral* world, just as God's acts of cooperation with events given in the world of sense are his miracles of the physical world.

God's *omnipresence* is closely bound up with *conservation*.[33] This omnipresence in fact consists simply in God's immediate operation in the duration of every thing in the world. The divine omnipresence is, in the first place, something *immediate*. In his conservation of substances, God does not act through intermediate causes. For if he did, then these causes would once again have to be substances which were his effects; consequently, one substance would have to operate in conserving the others, and thus one substance would be dependent on another. But one substance in the world cannot cause the existence of another. This was shown above, where we dealt with the impossibility of substances in the world standing *in commercio* with each other so as to be able to create each other. It is impossible too that substances could mutually contribute to the conservation of one another, or the duration of each other's existence. For creation and conservation are one and the same act. Further, God's

32. Kant's attitude toward Baumgarten's "MORAL OR SPECIAL CO-OPERATION OF GOD (*Concvrsvs Moralis seu Specialis*)" (*Metaphysica*, §960), is much more favorable. Kant does not think it impossible that moral conduct requires God's cooperation; but he does of course deny that we can ever *know* whether such events occur. (Cf. *Gesammelte Schriften*, vol. 6, p. 143; *Religion within the Limits of Reason Alone*, p. 134.)

33. "God is close to every monad in this world, and is inwardly present to every body. And it is by this motion (*momento*) that every creature is actual, Therefore, God is most omnipresent" (Baumgarten, *Metaphysica*, §956).

omnipresence is an *innermost* presence.[34] That is, God conserves what is substantial, the very inwardness of substances. For it is just this which is necessary for the duration of substances. And if God did not unceasingly actuate this inwardness and essential substantiality, then things in the world would all have to cease to be. Of course, we can think of a presence which is immediate but not inward. We have an example of such a thing in Newton's doctrine of the mutual attraction of all things in the world. Things attract each other immediately, or as he expressed it, in empty space. Consequently they operate reciprocally on one another and thus they are all present to one another. But they are not internal to each other. For this is only a case of reciprocal influence, that is, an operation on a thing's state or a modification of its changeable determinations in relation to other things. An inner presence, however, is an actuation of the durection of the very substance in a thing. Hence one cannot call conservation a "constant influence" of God on substances, as Baumgarten does.[35] For by speaking of an influence, he is saying that God conserves only the state of substances (their changeable determinations), and not the substances themselves. Hence, following Baumgarten, it could be asserted that matter is independent of God. So God's omnipresence is *immediate* and *inner* but not *local*. For it is impossible for a thing to be in two or more places at the same time, because then the thing would be external to itself (which is a contradiction). For example, suppose it is posited that thing A is in place a. Then A is wholly in a. If it is now said that it is in place b too, then it cannot be wholly in place a or in place b, but there must be a part of it in each place. Hence if it is to be asserted that God is in all places, then he has to be thought of as a composite being, as a mass extending throughout the whole world, something like the air. But then God would not exist wholly in any place in the

34. "What is proximately present as a whole and singly to the substantial parts of a thing, the same is called an INWARD PRESENCE to it. Now God is proximately present to all substantial parts of all bodies in this universe. Therefore, God is inwardly present to all bodies in this universe" (Baumgarten, *Metaphysica*, §955).

35. "Conservation is God's constant influence" (Baumgarten, *Metaphysica*, §951).

world; part of him would be in each place, just as the whole atmosphere is not in any place on the earth, but in each place there is always only a collection of little particles of air. Yet if God is the most perfect spirit, then he cannot be thought of as in space. For space is only a condition of the sensible appearance of things. Newton says somewhere that space is the *sensorium* of God's omnipresence.[36] Of course, one can think of such a *sensorium* in man, where the seat of the soul is located and where all the impressions of sense concur. This would be the soul's organ, the point from which it disperses its powers and operations into the whole body. But such a representation of God's omnipresence is most improper. For it would regard God as the soul of the world, and space as his *sensorium*. But this contradicts the concept of an independent God. For if God were the soul of the world, he would have to stand *in commercio* with the world and all the things in it. That is, he would not only operate on these things, but receive their operations as well. Or at least our only concept of a soul is that of an intelligence united with a body in such a way that both mutually influence one another. It is not easy to see how such a thing could be brought into agreement with the impassibility of a highest being. It would be better to say that space is a phenomenon of God's omnipresence, although even this expression is not entirely suitable. But it cannot be avoided on account of the poverty of language, which lacks words signifying such thoughts, not to mention expressing them clearly. But space is only an appearance of our senses, and a relation of things to each other. And the relation between things themselves is only possible insofar as God conserves them by his immediate and inner presence; thus he determines the place of each through his omnipresence. So to this extent God himself is the cause of space, and space is a phenomenon

36. "The first Contrivance of those very artificial Parts of Animals . . . and the Instinct of Brutes and Insects, can be the effect of nothing else than the Wisdom and Skill of a powerful ever-living Agent, who being in all Places, is more able by his Will to move the Bodies within his boundless uniform Sensorium, and thereby to form and reform the Parts of the Universe, than we are by our Will to move the Parts of our own Bodies" (Newton, *Opticks* [London, 1931], p. 403). Newton's conception of space as a manifestation of God reflects the influence of Henry More on his theology.

of his omnipresence. Hence God's omnipresence is not local, but virtual. That is, God's power operates constantly and everywhere on all things. In this way he conserves substances themselves, as well as governing their states. But we must be careful to keep ourselves away from all fanaticism in this representation. For although God's omnipresence expresses itself in each of us by the actuation of our very existence, this omnipresence cannot be felt by any of us, nor can any of us be certain for himself that God is operating in him in any particular case. For how am I to experience or be sensible of what is the cause of my own existence?

Of course if it were only a question of some change in my state, it might very well be possible for me to feel it. But no experience of the actuation of my own existence is possible. This reservation is of great importance, since it protects us from all fanatical madness and delusion.

If we affirm a *concursum divinum* as regards things, as well as events given in the world, then this is usually called a *concursum physicum*. But from what we have already said about God's cooperation with natural events, it can be seen how inappropriate it is to use this expression in place of divine conservation. For substances are certainly not coordinated with God, since they wholly depend on him as their *causa solitaria absolute prima*. So how can I regard substances as *concausae*, concurring with God in their own duration? Would I not then be asserting that their existence is not actuated by God, and that they do not have need of him alone for their duration, since he is only a cooperating cause of it?

It is equally wrong to posit a *concursum Dei* for events given in nature. For we can always think of a *causa proxima* for these events, operating in accordance with laws of nature; since otherwise they would *eo ipso* not be events given in nature. So it is likewise unthinkable that God, who is the *causa prima* of the whole of nature, might also operate as a *concausa* in each particular event. For then these events would only be so many miracles. Every case where God himself acts immediately is an exception to the rule of nature. But if God is to cooperate as a special *concausa* of every particular event given in nature, then every event would be an exception to the laws of nature. Or rather there would be no order at all in nature, because events given in it would not happen according to universal rules, but in each case God would have to give a *complementum ad sufficientiam* to anything which was to be set up in accordance with his will. But we could not think of such an imperfect world united to a wise author.

But now let us consider a *concursum moralem*, or God's free cooperation in the free actions of man. Such a thing cannot be comprehended in the nature of freedom, but at the same time it cannot be regarded as impossible. For it is a self-evident presupposition that every rational being could act contrary to God's plan, and consequently that such a being is free and independent of the entire mechanism of nature. Hence it is quite possible that God could also cooperate as a *concausa* of moral conduct, in order to make rational creatures use their freedom in a manner agreeable to his highest will.

God's providence is one single act. But we can think of it as having three separate functions: (1) *providing*, (2) *governing*, and (3) *directing*.[37] God's *providing* consists in the institution of the laws according to which the course of the world is to proceed. God's *governing* is the conservation of the course of the world in accordance with these laws. And God's *directing* is the determination of individual events in accordance with his decrees. Insofar as God's providence is benevolent, it is called his *care* for the world.[38] But all these expressions are infected by the concept of time in a manner likely to deceive us. Since we lack more suitable ones, we nevertheless must use them after separating all sensible limits from them.

God's providence is usually divided into *providentiam generalem* and *providentiam specialem*. The former means God's conservation of all types and kinds (*genera*). And the latter means his caring for *species*, a word used here in its juridical sense to

37. Providence = *Vorsehung* (*providentia*, cf. Baumgarten, *Metaphysica*, §974). Providing = *Providenz* (*providentia*). Governing = *Gubernation* (*gubernatio*, cf. Baumgarten, *Metaphysica*, §963). Directing = *Direction* (*dirigere strictius*, cf. Baumgarten, *Metaphysica*, §963).

38. Care for = *Vorsorge*.

signify individuals. At this point the expression *generalis* is to be distinguished from *universalis*, so that many exceptions may be made in a general providence.[39] For instance, it is as if we said of a king that *generaliter* (in general) he cares for his subjects. But such a concept of divine providence is obviously wholly anthropomorphic. For such a provision is extremely imperfect, and in fact could only be found in a being who has to be acquainted through experience with what is needed. But experience only furnishes an aggregate, and hence the rules which are abstracted from it can never be universal, because some of the possible perceptions are always lacking. Consequently, it is impossible for every law whose beneficence rests on principles of experience to suit every individual in the state and to work equally for the well-being of all and the common utility. For how could the lord of a country be acquainted with every single one of his subjects and with all the circumstances under which his laws might be of great advantage to one, but detrimental to another? But God has no need of experience at all. He knows everything a priori, because he himself created everything he cares for; and everything is possible only through him. Hence God formulated the laws governing the world in light of a thorough acquaintance with every single event which would be given in the course of it. And in the establishment of the world's course he certainly had the greatest possible perfection in view, because God himself is the all-wise and is all in all. For certainly in his omniscience he foresaw every possible individual before there was anything at all, as well as every *genus*. And in actualizing them he cared for their existence as well as their welfare, through the establishment of suitable laws. Hence because God knows everything a priori, his providence is *universalis*, or general enough to comprehend everything, *genera*, *species*, and individuals. In one

39. Part of Kant's problem in this passage is due to the fact that the German word *allgemein* means both "general" and "universal," and hence translates both *generalis* and *universalis*. *Allgemein* will be translated both as "general" and as "universal," as the context dictates. Kant has to indicate the difference less directly, as when he distinguishes what happens merely generally (*allgemein*) or "on the whole" (*im Ganzen*) from what is "general enough" (*so allgemein*) as to comprehend genera, species and individuals. The latter is "*real* universality" (*reale Allgemeinheit*) or "wholly universal" (*ganz allgemein*).

glance God surveys all of existence and he conserves it by his power. This universality of divine providence is not a logical universality, like universal rules we draw up in order to classify the characteristics of things. Rather, it is a *real* universality; for God's understanding is intuitive, and only ours is discursive. Hence it is foolish to think of a divine providence on the whole (*generalis*) as coming from a highest being; for such a being could not fail to know the totality in every single part. Rather, God's providence is wholly universal (*universalis*), and thus the distinction of a *providentia generali* from a *providentia speciali* collapses of itself.

Since every event given in the world is directed by God's supreme will, the divine direction is partly *orderly* and partly *extraordinary*.[40] The former consists in God's setting up an order in nature, so that its laws accord with what he decrees for the world. And God's extraordinary direction consists in the fact that he sometimes determines in accordance with his aims that individual events should not correspond to the order of nature. It is not at all impossible that in even the best world the powers of nature may sometimes require the immediate cooperation of God in order to bring about certain great purposes. It is not impossible that the Lord of nature might at times communicate to it a *complementum ad sufficientiam* in order to carry out his plan. For who is so presumptuous that he wants to know how everything God intends for the world could be attained in accordance with universal laws, and without his extraordinary direction?

Hence God can use natural causes merely as means for bringing about this or that event which he has placed before himself as an end, and for the sake of the greater perfection of the whole. These exceptions to the rules of nature may be necessary because without them God might not be able to put many great aims into practice in the usual course of nature. Only we must guard ourselves from trying to determine, without further instruction, whether God's direction is to be found in this or that case. It is enough that everything is subject to God's direction. This is sufficient for us to place an immeasurable trust in God.

40. Orderly = *ordentlich*. Extraordinary = *ausserordentlich*.

Nevertheless, not everything *happens* through divine direction, even if everything is *subject* to it. For any event which is produced immediately by the divine will is a miracle, and an effect of God's extraordinary direction. Now every miracle either was woven by God into the laws of nature during the creation of the world, or else he works it in the course of the world in order to bring about some necessary aim of his. In neither case should we ever expect a miracle; though we cannot deny them either. To reassure ourselves in the face of life's accidents, we may think of every event as fundamentally a consequence of God's government and direction. What does it matter whether these events happen in accordance with the order of nature or in an extraordinary way? For everything is subject to God's care.

We must never regard prayer as a means to getting our own way; if a prayer concerns our corporeal advantage, we ought to say it both with a trust in God's wisdom and with a submission to this wisdom. The greatest utility of prayer is indisputably a *moral* one, because through prayer both thankfulness and resignation toward God become effective in us. But the greatest caution and care are necessary if we are going to investigate whether this or that event is one of God's immediate purposes, which he has contrived or effected in an extraordinary way. For we must not, at the bidding of a lazy reason, derive anything from God as its immediate cause when sharper reflection might convince us that it was only a natural effect; and even if all our researches on this score should be in vain, it is still the case that our fruitless seeking fulfills our great calling and furthers the cultivation of our reason.

In the course of our discussion of the truth that God created the whole world for the best, it was necessary to reply to the objection asking how moral evil could be found in a best world. But we still have the duty of showing why God has not prevented evil, in view of the fact that everything is subject to his government.

The possibility of deviating from the moral law must belong to every creature. For it is unthinkable that any creature could be without needs and limits. God alone is unlimited. But if every creature has needs and deficiencies, then impulses of sense (which are derived from these needs) must be able to seduce him to forsake morality. It is self-evident that we are speaking here only of free creatures, for there is no morality for irrational creatures. If man is to be a free creature and be responsible for the development and cultivation of his abilities and predispositions, then it must also be within his power to follow or to shun the laws of morality. Man's use of his freedom has to depend on him, even if it should wholly conflict with the plan God designed for the moral world. God could have given man overriding powers and motives sufficient to make him a member of the great kingdom of ends by divine decree. Hence if God does not prevent evil in the world, this never sanctions evil; it only permits it.

III. God as Ruler of the World

God is the only ruler of the world. He governs as a monarch, but not as a despot; for he wills to have his commands observed out of love, and not out of servile fear.[41] Like a father, he orders what is good for us, and does not command out of mere arbitrariness, like a tyrant. God even demands of us that we reflect on the reason for his commandments, and he insists on our observing them because he wants first to make us worthy of happiness and then make us participate in it. God's will is benevolence, and his purpose is what is best. If God commands something for which we cannot see the reason, then this is because of the limitations of our knowledge, and not because of the nature of the commandment itself. God carries out his rulership of the world *alone*. For he surveys everything with one glance. And certainly he may often use wholly incomprehensible means to carry out his benevolent aims.

Since God governs everything, we are warranted in assuming a teleological connection in nature. For governing presupposes purposes, and God's government presupposes the wisest and

41. Baumgarten describes God not only as a "monarch" but also as a "despot," since he has not only "supreme power" over them but also "plenary power" (*Metaphysica*, §974). Kant finds the terms *despotes* and *monarchia despotica* morally offensive as applied to God.

best. Of course in many cases our efforts to discover these purposes will be in vain, because the true purposes of the highest understanding are so concealed from our insight that we cannot track them down. Great care is required on our part if we are not to take some event in nature to be one of God's purposes when it is really either only a means or a by-product of a higher purpose. But even if we sometimes engage in these researches without success, still we have exercised our reason and at least discovered something. And even if we go wholly wrong, no greater harm results than that we take something to be the work of intention when it is only a mechanism of nature. A need of our own reason requires that we search everywhere for universal laws ordering certain given events. For in this way we bring unity and harmony into our knowledge of nature, instead of destroying all order in nature, as we would do if we regarded every single thing in the world as an effect of God's special providence.

In the same way, we can also think of events in world history, which are consequences of human freedom, as conjoined with and carried out by God's government according to a plan. But here too, according to the nature of our reason, we have to hold on to the universal, and not try to determine how divine providence has proven itself effective in particular cases.

It is true that for God's understanding, which knows everything intuitively, the whole is fundamentally a whole only insofar as it arises out of the particular. Consequently, divine providence is fully universal, so that it includes every individual in its plan. But it would be perverse of us, and contrary to our discursive reason, if we too tried to rise from the particular to the universal and survey the whole in the same way. The nature of our reason lays on us the duty of first meditating on universal laws and then, as far as possible, of grasping every individual and even every species under them. This is the way we can form some sketch of the whole, and although it is certainly very incomplete, it is nevertheless sufficient for our needs.

What Baumgarten says about God's decrees is obviously only a human representation. For in God the decree and its execution are one.[42] But it is necessary to our concept, as long as we think of it in a worthy manner. Yet an *absolutum decretum* is absolutely improper as regards God.[43] For such a thing would make of God not only a despot, but a complete tyrant; as if, without any regard to the worthiness of his subjects, he elected some to happiness and condemned the others straightway to reprobation, providing all sorts of remedies to the one and withdrawing from the other every power and opportunity to make themselves worthy of happiness, in order to do all this with propriety and an appearance of right. It would be almost unthinkable that any man with a heart and insight could come to such dishonorable thoughts about God, unless it is assumed for their honor's sake either that they have not thought over the terrible consequences of such corrupt doctrines, or have not shunned them merely out of stupefaction. For such teachings would turn the concept of God into a scandal, and all morality into a figment of the brain. Such views also conflict wholly with the idea of human freedom, since in this way all actions can be considered merely to accord with the necessity of nature. Hence speculative philosophers may always be forgiven for having fallen on such representations, since human freedom and its possibility will always be something insoluble for them. But in any theology which is to be a principle of religion, it is both puzzling and senseless to make such concepts of God one's foundation. As an appearance, the human soul certainly belongs to the series of natural things. But if it is free as an *intelligence*, then it has to depend on the soul itself whether it will be worthy or unworthy of happiness.

42. Kant apparently has in mind here Baumgarten's threefold distinction between (1) the *propositum* in which God represents the best complex of compossible beings, (2) the *praevisio* in which he knows it *as* the best possible world, and (3) the *decretum* through which this best world receives its existence. Since these three "mental acts" of God are distinguished as if they followed in a temporal order, Kant objects to the discussion as "merely a human representation." But Baumgarten himself admits that this account of God's decree of the best world is only "a way in which it may be conceived according to a human fashion" (*Metaphysica*, §976).

43. Kant is agreeing with Baumgarten's insistence that God's decrees are not "absolute" (i.e. unconditional). Both reject the doctrines of eternal reprobation and predestination which seem to follow from this *absolutismus theologicas* (Baumgarten, *Metaphysica*, §980).

Insofar as its object is the reprobation of one whole part of mankind, this doctrine of predestination presupposes an *immoral* order of nature. For the doctrine asserts that in the case of some men, the circumstances of their life are so ordered and conjoined that they could not but be unworthy of blessedness. Hence simply according to the order of nature, these unfortunates have to be sacrifices to misery. But how could such a thing be compatible with the concept of a benevolent, wise, and holy creator and governor of the world? It is one of the great advantages provided by the doctrine of God from the point of view of our knowledge and reassurance, that this doctrine brings the kingdom of nature into exact harmony with the kingdom of ends. It is from this doctrine that we are to infer that the whole order of nature is arranged in accordance with God's purposes, and agrees with these purposes. But then are we to suppose that one of God's purposes is the misery of a part of his creatures?

God's governance of the world in accordance with moral principles is an assumption without which all morality would have to break down. For if morality cannot provide me with the prospect of satisfying my needs, then it cannot command anything of me either. Hence it is also necessary that God's will should not be made the principle of rational morality. For in this way we could never be sure what God had in mind for the world. How can I know by reason and speculation what God's will is, and what it consists in? Without morality to help me here, I would be on a slippery path, surrounded by mountains which afford me no prospect. And I would be in great danger of having my foot slip, or of wandering lost in a labyrinth, because no clear horizon ever meets my eye.

The knowledge of God, therefore, must complete morality, but it must not determine whether something is morally good, or a duty for me. This I have to judge from the nature of things, in accordance with a possible system of ends; and I must be just as certain of it as I am that a triangle has three angles. But in order to provide my heart with conviction, import, and emphasis, I have need of a God who will make me participate in happiness in accordance with these eternal and unchangeable laws, if I am worthy of it. In the same way, the knowledge of

God and his providence is the goal of our natural sciences. It must be the crown of all our endeavors, but not the principle from which we derive every single event before we have sought the universal laws applying to it.

Fourth Section: Revelation

Baumgarten defines *revelationem latius dictam* as *significationem mentis divinae creaturis a Deo factam*. But this definition of revelation in general is *angustior suo definito*.[44] For divine revelation must be able to furnish us with convincing knowledge of God's existence and properties as well as of his will. The former have to be the motive and incentive impelling us to fulfill the latter. Revelation is either *external* or *inward*. An external revelation can be of two kinds: either (1) through works, or (2) through words. Inward divine revelation is God's revelation to us through our own reason. It must precede all other revelation and serve as a judge of external revelation. It has to be the touchstone by which I know whether an external revelation is really from *God*; and it must give me proper concepts of him. For as we have seen above, nature by itself can never give me a complete and determinate concept of God unless I bring reason to its aid. Nature teaches us to fear that being (or more than one) which might have produced the world, but it does not teach us to honor and love God without flattery and as a being possessing every perfection. Yet there is little to be gained as regards the confirmation or awakening of morality from the concept of God nature gives me, if I make it into a principle of religion. For such a concept of God is a concept of a very powerful being, but I could hardly come to know God as a benevolent being through nature, on account of the apparent conflict of purposes in the world. In short, it is not a concept of God as a most perfect being that

44. "Revelation in the wider sense is the mental signification made by God to his creatures" (Baumgarten, *Metaphysica*, §982). Kant objects that this definition is "narrower than what it defines," perhaps because he thinks it implies that revelation so defined can furnish only knowledge of God's will, without guaranteeing that it is the will of a supremely perfect being, and thus a will deserving of our rational obedience.

nature provides, it is only a concept of him as a very perfect one. But then of what use is the natural concept of God as a whole? Certainly none other than the use actually made of it by most peoples: as a terrifying picture of fantasy, and a superstitious object of ceremonial adoration and hypocritical high praise.

But now suppose that prior to physicotheology my reason has already taught me that God is all in all; and that in accordance with my knowledge of moral laws I have gained insight into the concept of God as a being who governs the world according to the highest morality. Then in this case my knowledge of nature will serve admirably to give the pure concepts of my understanding greater intuitive appeal and to make a stronger impression on the sensible man. I will no longer be in danger of forming an incomplete concept of God from mere nature. For now I have already received from my reason a thoroughly determinate concept; and by means of this concept I can judge all God's works in this world insofar as he has revealed himself in them. In just the same way, the revelation of God through words presupposes an inward divine revelation through my own reason. For words are only sensible signs of my thoughts. So how by means of them am I to attain to a wholly pure concept of God? But if my own reason has already abstracted such a concept from things, if with the help of morality it has already come to a wholly determinate concept of God, then I have a norm in accordance with which I can assess and explain the verbal expressions of God's revelation. Even if God were to make an immediate appearance, I would still need rational theology as a presupposition. For how am I to be certain that it is God himself who has appeared to me, or only another powerful being? Thus I have need of a pure idea of the understanding, an idea of a most perfect being, if I am not to be blinded and led astray. Thus we can have no correct insight into the external revelation of God, and we can make no right use of it, until we have made a wholly rational theology our property. But on the other hand an external divine revelation can be an occasion for man to come for the first time to pure concepts of God which are pure concepts of the understanding; and it can also give him the opportunity to search for these concepts. A verbal revelation will always become more and more a matter of learning the longer it lasts, even if in the beginning it was something quite simple. For with time it becomes a matter of tradition, whether it is transmitted verbally or in writing. And then there can be only a few whose learning is broad enough that they can go back to its very first origins and carefully test its genuineness. Here the religion of reason always has to remain the substratum and foundation of every investigation. It is according to this religion that the value of verbal revelation must be determined. So it must precede every other revelation and serve as a yardstick.

In rational theology there are many *credenda* which reason itself urges us to assume; and it is an important duty for us to believe them with conviction. The object of this knowledge—God—is an object of such a kind that there can be no scientific knowledge of it, since it transcends every possible experience and belongs to the intelligible world. For I can have scientific knowledge only of what I myself experience. But as regards our morality, it is very good that our knowledge is not scientific knowledge but faith. For in this way the fulfillment of my duty will be far purer and more unselfish. But the matters of faith pertaining to rational religion extend their obligation to the whole human species; for every rational being must assume them unfailingly from a moral point of view, even if he cannot prove them with apodictic certainty.

Now it can be asked whether there are also *credenda* given in a higher revelation, which have to be assumed even though reason does not recognize the necessity of believing them. But reason can *neither deny nor prove* the possibility of such things. In the first place, no man can hold it impossible that in order to bring the human species to perfection in its vocation, God might have given men certain truths necessary to their happiness in a higher revelation, even though reason, through its own cultivation, can never attain to insight regarding them. For who would dare to specify the plan or the means by which God might help men to become what their vocation determines them to be?

But on the other hand, my reason has just as little insight as to how something not lying in reason but transcending all reason could be necessary to the welfare of mankind. Thus a pagan philosopher once said: *Quod supra nos, nihil ad nos*.[45] The precise knowledge of and adherence to the path reason prescribes is all that God himself teaches to make us worthy of any higher insight which might be provided to supplement reason's deficiencies. For how could I reckon on additional gifts and presents even before I have applied and used what I am already endowed with?

Mysteries, properly so called, are those doctrines which are not to be made public.[46] So in general they are truths whose possibility reason cannot see into, but which still have to be assumed from other causes. There are many natural mysteries. But there are also many mysteries in rational religion. An example is the absolute necessity of God. For reason is urged for its own sake to believe in God's necessity, but reason comes to a standstill as soon as it is a question of gaining insight into the possibility of such a thing. A further mystery is this. A just God in his benevolence can distribute happiness only according to the object's worthiness to be happy. Yet he can make man happy even when he finds himself unworthy of happiness, since before the bar of conscience his best striving is never adequate to the whole of the moral law. Here our reason is profoundly silent. For even if it just says: "Do as much good as you can," this is still a long way from being sufficient to reassure me. For where is the man who can determine how much good he can do? Where is the man bold enough to say: "I have done everything I could"? I cannot depend on God's beneficence here. For my reason has to think of God's judgment as supremely just, limiting benevolence by his strict holiness, so that no one unworthy might participate in it. It is an impenetrable mystery for my reason what kind of means God has here to replace what is lacking in my worthiness to be happy. It is enough that I have a duty to strive as much as possible to act in accordance with the

45. "What is above us is nothing to us." The classical proverb is often attributed to Socrates.

46. "Holy mysteries are things set above the reason of creatures, and included in the objects of holy faith" (Baumgarten, *Metaphysica*, §906).

moral law. It is in this way that I will make myself susceptible and worthy of these means. Hence, as we have said, it cannot be denied that mysteries are possible in God's verbal revelation. And *it does not belong to rational theology to say whether or not there actually are such mysteries*.

Appendix: A History of Natural Theology, according to Meiners' *Historia doctrinae de uno vero Deo*[1]

In their reflections about what the human understanding has always known of God, men have fallen into two extremes; and these extremes have also been used as principles of rational theology, accounting for a variety of systems: (1) Some have tried to deny reason any capacity to know anything true and reliable about God. (2) Others have praised their reason so highly that they have tried to derive from it all the knowledge of God which is necessary for man.

The former have had need of some verbal revelation from God at every instant; while the latter despised all such revelation. Both have appealed to history, but both were in error. For if we go to work with sincerity and an impartial spirit of investigation, we find that reason does in fact have the capacity to form a morally determinate concept of God, a concept which is as complete as possible for it. But on the other hand we have to admit that from a variety of causes this pure concept of the Deity is not easy to find in any ancient people. What was to blame for this was not reason itself, but only the obstacles which stood in the way of reason's making use of its ability in this respect. But reason certainly has no right to be proud of this ability, and its

1. Christoph Meiners (1747–1810), was a prolific German writer on a wide variety of historical topics. The *Historia doctrinae de uno vero Deo* (1780) was the first of his many writings on the history of religions, culminating in his two volume *Allgemeine kritische Geschichte der Religionen* (1806).

own relation to the infinite. If it is honest and free of prejudice, it still has to discover many deficiencies and weaknesses even in the most complete system of theology possible for it. And certainly it must not boast about its knowledge of God. If a higher revelation has disclosed some clearer insight into its relation to God, reason should accept this revelation with thanksgiving and use it rather than rejecting it. It is true that the moral concept of God reason gives us is so simple and obvious to the ordinary human understanding that not much cultivation is required for faith in a supreme governor of the world. And it is necessary too that any knowledge which is to interest the whole human species must be intelligible to every man. But a person would have to be very little acquainted with the errors of man's understanding if he seriously asserted that this concept of God is safe from misinterpretation and disfigurement by hypocritical speculation. Hence it is necessary to keep it safe from corruption by means of profound reflection and a pointed critique of all speculative reason.

The principal cause for the corruption of the concept of God was that men had very little knowledge of morality which was pure and certain. They commonly took their own advantage to be their duty, and this eliminated all true moral value from their actions. Or else they grounded the beauty and magnitude of virtue on a mere feeling, and not on a principle determined and firmly establishing free rationality as the unchangeable norm and the condition for all its obligations. Hence they were not acquainted with any moral need to postulate a most perfect lawgiver for the world.

Only from a speculative standpoint did the ancients assume a supreme cause, in order to complete the series of causes and effects. But since nature can only lead us to a powerful and intelligent author, and never to one who has all reality, the ancients fell into polytheism and endlessly multiplied their gods in accordance with these merely natural concepts. And even if a few for the sake of greater harmony assumed only one single cause for the world, still their concept was fundamentally only a deistic one, because they were not thinking of a highest moral author and governor of the world, but only of a supreme original source for everything. For fundamentally no ancient people had any concept of God which could be used as a foundation for morality. On this point, Meiners is certainly correct. But he is mistaken if he believes that they did not come upon such a concept because a great deal of culture and an acquaintance with science is required for it. This cannot possibly be said of the simple moral concept of God. For almost nothing is easier in itself than the thought of a being who is supreme above all and who is all in all. It is much more difficult to divide perfection, and to ascribe one perfection to one being and another perfection to another, because one never knows how much each is to be given. But we must concede that if the concept of the divine is also to be secured from the side of speculation, there must first be some knowledge of it, and some scientific reflection about it. But this reflection was not necessary before human wit and sagacity had begun to venture speculating about the divine. And some culture was required for that.

The Egyptians had only a deistic concept of God, or rather a wretched polytheistic one. The established belief that all of Greek science and culture came from Egypt, though it is founded on the sayings of Herodotus, is really a prejudice. For the situation and constitution of the country, the tyranny of the pharaohs and the usurpation of the priests, must instead have formed this people into a gloomy, melancholy, and ignorant mass. It is also wholly unproven that the Egyptians had surpassed any other people of that time in any field of useful knowledge (unless we are to count soothsaying and the interpretation of dreams). Instead, some sciences (such as geometry) must already have been available to men at this time, so that they could populate their land and make it habitable. For without these sciences the annual flooding of the Nile would have destroyed all their property. Besides, their priests truly monopolized all the arts they might have had and never let them serve the common utility, since otherwise their own reputation and their avarice would have suffered shipwreck. The most credible historians of the ancient world inform us as to which sciences the

Greeks invented, and when. Among them we find those very ones which some, through a delusion, have believed they received from the Egyptians.

The worship of animals, as regards its origin, can probably be explained tolerably well. Perhaps in the beginning these animals were merely part of the coat of arms used by each city to distinguish itself from the others. Subsequently the peoples retained them, but finally, blinded by superstition, they assumed them as protective gods and worshipped them. It does not hold of these peoples (as Hume, in his *Natural Religion*, has quite correctly said of polytheism) that they were tolerant.[2] For if one city among them had a protective god directly opposed to another (for example, one being a dog and the other a cat), then this alone made enemies of their inhabitants. For they believed that one deity would always try to encroach on the other's power and prevent much good which it would otherwise have given its clients.

The Greeks and certain others were sufficiently tolerant of other heathen peoples, and of one another as well. For they found their own deities in those of other peoples; only the names were different, since for the most part the attributes were the same. But it was on account of this that all heathen peoples held a terrible hatred for the Jews, because the Deity of this people was elevated above all of theirs, and his nature and will had nothing in common with their gods. Hence it was also natural that monotheism (and the Jews who held it) should be so intolerant of all heathens.

The Persians, Indians, and other heathen peoples of antiquity had a theology far more passable than that of the Egyptians. It is true that they prayed to many gods. But the concepts that they formed of these gods were nevertheless in some measure worthy of the object, even if they were quite corrupt. In general we must admit that nearly all these peoples probably had at least a dim thought of a supreme Deity above their idols, as a primary source from which everything (including the lower gods) origi-

2. Hume, *The Natural History of Religion*, Section IX (Stanford, 1967), pp. 48–51.

nated; but it was wholly unconcerned about the world. Even now this is still the representation of God held by some heathens. And since their concepts of God were abstracted only from the world, it was also wholly natural that they regarded him by analogy with nature as a fertile cause from which everything had emanated.

Among the Greeks we find no natural theology earlier than the time of the so-called seven sages. But for a long time their concepts of God were only deistic, until finally Anaxagoras and Socrates made God the foundation of morality. But by then morality itself had already been founded on secure principles. So it was easy to establish a moral concept of God, the only one truly useful for mankind. But as soon as men knew God as a principle of nature and began speculating about him, then it was easy for them to be led astray again. Plato and Aristotle did maintain a pure and morally determinate concept of God, because they applied it only in behalf of morality. But Epicurus and others wanted to found the natural sciences on this concept as well, and so they nearly gave up morality or else lost themselves in skepticism. For a great deal of knowledge and caution would have been required of them here, if they were going to unite science with morality and yet not be led astray by the apparent conflict of purposes in the world. But it must be admitted that Epicurus preserved a concept of the Deity which is quite pure, considered from a speculative point of view. Yet the greatest advantage of this was lost to him and his disciples. For such a God cannot be used as an incentive to morality. The stoics probably had the purest concept of God, and they did apply it to practical aims. But they could not raise themselves far enough to regard God as the creator of the world. For even if they did use the term *creator* of him, if we consider this precisely, we will see that only the concept of an architect was combined with this term. They always assumed a matter co-eternal with God, from which Jupiter (a name designating not the poetic god of thunder, but the highest Deity above everything) had formed and arranged the things of the world. For they carefully distinguished fate from necessity and understood by the former nothing but

God's government and care for the world. Yet in order to justify the supremely perfect God against all the ill and evil found in the world, they pushed the blame for them onto the unfitness of matter, which could not always be used for the supreme aims of the architect.

How fortunate we are that neither moral nor physical evil can shake our faith in one God who governs the world in accordance with moral laws!

Index

Library of Congress Cataloging in Publication Data
(For library cataloging purposes only)

Kant, Immanuel, 1724–1804.
Lectures on philosophical theology.
Translation of Immanuel Kants Vorlesungen über die philosphische Religionslehre.
Includes index.
1. Philosophical theology—Addresses, essays, lectures. I. Wood, Allen W., II. Clark, Gertrude M. III. Title.
B2794.V642E54 1978 200'.1 78-58034
ISBN 0-8014-1199-8

RANDOM: no design.

→ The perfect state would need to be constituted of an aggregate of perfect individuals (GODS) — not genetically possible.